Your Fate Is
in Your Hands

Your Fate Is in Your Hands

Using the Principles of Palmistry to Change Your Life

DONNA MCCUE

WITH STACEY DONOVAN

POCKET BOOKS
New York   London   Toronto   Sydney   Singapore

To protect the privacy of clients, individual names and identifying characteristics have been altered for use in this book. Any resemblance to living persons is strictly coincidental.

The epigraph to Chapter Fifteen (on page 234) is from a poem by Wendy Huemme-Rodriguez and is printed with the kind permission of the author.

An *Original* Publication of POCKET BOOKS

 POCKET BOOKS, a division of Simon & Schuster Inc.
1230 Avenue of the Americas, New York, NY 10020

Copyright © 2000 by Donna McCue

Library of Congress Cataloging-in-Publication Data

McCue, Donna.
    Your fate is in your hands : using the principles of palmistry to change
your life / Donna McCue, with Stacey Donovan.
        p. cm.
    Includes bibliographical references.
    ISBN 0-671-03877-X
    1. Palmistry. I. Donovan, Stacey. II. Title.
BF921 .M18 2000
133.6—dc21   99-055093

First Pocket Books trade paperback printing January 2000

10 9 8 7 6 5 4 3 2 1

POCKET and colophon are registered trademarks
of Simon & Schuster Inc.

Cover design by Brigid Pearson
Book design by Jessica Shatan
Illustrations by Charlotte Sherwood

Printed in the U.S.A.

To my loving family—
my husband, Larry,
and my two sons, Daniel and Alex
—*Donna McCue*

CONTENTS

FOREWORD

As I was preparing to write this book, I received a phone call from a close friend named Jane. After owning a jewelry store for eight years, she had just sold the business and was able to buy a new, luxury car for the first time in her life. She wanted to christen it by driving me into New York City for lunch, and I gladly agreed. The car was beautiful with its soft leather seats, walnut interior, and a sound system that made you feel as if Barbra Streisand were singing in the backseat.

We were having an enjoyable ride until we arrived in Queens, where we encountered heavy traffic due to an accident. In order to sidestep the traffic, Jane decided to leave the Long Island Expressway and travel the side roads to the Midtown Tunnel. I was hesitant as she sped off the expressway and asked her if she knew where she was going. "Not at all," she said happily, "but the car does." She then touched some buttons on the bottom of a small screen that sat between the driver's and passenger's seats, and a map appeared on the screen.

Jane pressed the buttons again and the map grew more and more particularized, eventually displaying our precise location. After following the little map, we ended up at the Midtown Tunnel in no time. It was truly amazing. When I asked how it worked, Jane explained that the car was equipped with something called a Global Positioning System, which communicated by satellite to a larger system that kept track of the car, and ultimately, was able to guide us to our destination.

That electronic road map is just one of the new technologies we have available to us as the new century begins. The Global Positioning System impressed me so because it reminded me of just how significantly the age-old science and "technology" of palmistry has guided people for thousands of years—in the very same manner as its more modern counterpart. Because I have spent my entire adult life studying the hand, I have come to realize that it is the human "road map," leading us to the deepest truths in our lives. And that is my reason for writing this book, to share the most important insights I have gleaned from my many years of hand analysis. We are in possession of our own road maps; it is we who turn here or there, inviting spiritual guidance and direction to enter our lives; and therefore, it is we who hold fate in our hands.

Many of us do not know that the lines of our hands are constantly changing, offering us new information and continual feedback about ourselves. This makes it apparent that it is up to each and every one of us to follow the changing course of our truest selves—or not. In this book, then, as you begin to understand the *lines* and *markings* in your own hand, you will learn how to identify your own truths and chart the changes of your circumstances.

As you are introduced to the specific locations and meanings of the hand's various characteristics, your own hand will soon become your ongoing visual aid, continually helping you become aware of any blocks and challenges that may face you on the road of your life. By reading about my own quest for the truth in my life and the experiences of my clients in these pages, you will soon discover that you can unblock negative patterns in your path and thereby become free to experience clarity, spirituality, and wholeness in your life.

Your Fate Is
in Your Hands

Just Knowing: The Beginning

My first psychic experience occurred when I was four years old. This hardly surprises me now, as children are so often able to sense more about the world around them than adults. In part, this is because children possess a purity and clarity of understanding that is sadly and largely lost to their elders. Too, I believe it is because children experience life without question, which keeps them naturally closer to a pure and honest psychic state that most adults, who have retreated behind the shields of self-consciousness and social conformity, lose.

It was an icy winter day in Syracuse, New York, and I told my mother that my father would come home that day from a business trip—even though he was not expected until the next day. At first, my mother had no reason to believe my prediction, but my father *did* come home, in spite of the snow that had blanketed the city and roads. Shortly thereafter, I mentioned to my mother that a neighbor of ours was going to have a heart attack. Two days later, he did. More

and more, my mother came to depend on my pronounce-
ments. Though I was at a loss to explain why, somehow I just
knew what was going to happen to those around me.

This gift of "just knowing," as I called it in my early years,
worked as a defensive device in my life. My father, consumed
by work pressures and a stressful marriage, exercised his
power on those weaker and smaller than himself, and my
growing intuition was a means of protecting myself—just as a
small animal uses all its senses to protect itself from a larger
predator. My "just knowing" manifested itself in chills that
traveled up and down my arms and legs, a sensation I experience to this day.

And so I "knew" when he was coming home because I did
not want him to; the instant I knew, my hands would clench
into fists.

When I was eight years old, I was finally old enough to
take the bus alone into downtown Syracuse to my dance
lessons, which I loved. Though it was only a fifteen-minute
ride, it was long enough to make me feel magically grown-
up, as if I might actually be able to leave behind my troubles
at home. Meeting Miss Augustine on the bus one morning
made me feel even more hopeful. She was a sleek, polished
businesswoman in her early thirties, and I could not help but
stare at her beautiful hands the instant I saw them. Her fingers held rings that boasted sparkling diamonds, and the tips
of her long, elegant fingers were painted a stunning bright
red. I had never seen such well-cared-for hands, and I hid my
own hands in my pockets, suddenly ashamed of my badly bit-
ten nails—a habit my entire family engaged in. As subsequent
Saturdays arrived, Miss Augustine, on her way to her
women's accessory shop, would save me a seat on the bus.
One morning, she caught me staring at her nails and smiled.
"If you can stop biting *your* nails," she said, "I will give you
some nail polish of your own. You can even pick the color."

From that moment on, I was determined to stop biting my

nails. Even though it was hard, my desire for beautiful red nail polish like Miss Augustine's thwarted my bad habit. More than anything, I wanted to be as beautiful as Miss Augustine. As the weeks went by, my nails grew, and I could not wait to see her again. One morning, Miss Augustine beamed proudly as she handed me a beautifully wrapped package. I tried to keep from tearing the paper as I opened the gift. Inside was not only a bottle of red polish, but a small manicure set in a red leather case. After returning home and showing my parents the wonderful present, my father immediately tossed the polish into the trash can. Of course, I held on to my manicure set for dear life, and Miss Augustine took the time to show me how to use it. When she asked me where the polish was, I told her that I had to wait until I was older to wear it. She nodded understandingly, as I knew she would.

Unfortunately, not everyone believed in my "just knowing." In fact, when I became desperate for someone outside my family to understand my situation, I was swiftly rebuffed.

I was thirteen and had begun to feel increasingly alone, sad, and depressed. Over the course of my childhood, my father had become more violent and abusive. At the time, I could not understand the origins of his anger, but I instinctively knew that I had to learn to protect myself from it. One summer day, I went to see a social worker in downtown Syracuse, to tell her what was happening at home. When I finished describing the latest episode with my father and told her how afraid I was, she looked at me and said, "Go home like a good girl." But home was the last place I wanted to be. *Was I crazy?* I wondered.

Repeatedly, my father told me I was "stupid" and "no good." Was that true? As a way of staying out of the house, I started baby-sitting for a family down the block, doing laundry and making meals for the five kids. Though they paid me a mere twenty dollars for forty hours of work, I did not care. I saved my money. I knew there were things I could do if I had money. I knew there would be a future.

A month later I returned to the social worker's office for a follow-up visit, though I was not exactly sure why I had agreed to go. It was hot and muggy, and my thighs rubbed together beneath my girdle as I walked along Main Street. When I stopped to rub a blister my new loafers had caused, I spotted a sign in the window of the old Syracuse Hotel: Palm Reading by Florry Nadall, author of *Pen in Hand: A Simplified Guide to "Instant" Handwriting Analysis*. I thought, *Why go to the social worker when I could have my palm read?*—reasoning that if I could learn what the future had in store for me, I could better cope with my turbulent life at home.

Usually, when my spirits needed a lift, I would buy something like false eyelashes and movie magazines, but now I was walking into the Syracuse Hotel for my first palm reading. At five feet tall, I weighed one hundred twenty pounds, and I was wearing one of my mother's dresses, which made me feel one hundred years old. My self-esteem was lower than low. I walked through the hotel door, both frightened and excited. Inside, Florry Nadall sat behind a velvet-covered table, looking like a cross between kindly Aunt Bea from *The Andy Griffith Show* and softhearted Mrs. Cleaver from *Leave It to Beaver*, her gentle eyes welcoming me beneath a halo of soft yellow hair. I was immediately calmed by her presence. It did not matter that the reading cost a full week's baby-sitting pay—I would have given her my entire savings to feel the least bit hopeful and know what my future would bring. Would I become a movie star? Would I be famous? Would I ever stop wearing a girdle?

Florry inhaled slowly and studied my palm for a few moments, then told me that I had the natural aptitude of a performer and would be in the public eye as a result of my work. She continued to say that I would be restless and would travel to foreign countries, and by my late thirties, I would marry and have two children. She finished by predicting that I would have two homes and, at some point, I would live on an island. The very last thing she told me was that, in a previous life, my father's violence and rage nearly killed me.

How could she possibly know so much about me? I wondered, marveling at her knowledge of the most private details of my life.

Many years have passed since Florry Nadall read my palm. Incredibly, everything she said about my life eventually came true. Her comments about my father *felt* true—though, of course, I could not prove what happened in a former life. Meeting Florry was nothing like the harsh, confusing experience of talking to the social worker, who simply denied my reality. Florry offered me reassurance as well as sorely needed answers. After our meeting, I felt a huge rush of relief, though at the time the idea of marrying and having kids was the last thing I could envision for myself. That day, I left the hotel and splurged on a butterscotch sundae at Woolworth's. "Hold the nuts!" I said. Because I was not crazy at all. I looked in awe at my hands, unusually open and relaxed.

Now, I wondered, *what would become of me?*

As a result of my early experiences, one of the things I have discovered is that the truth can, indeed, be difficult to accept. Another thing I have learned is that growth is often accompanied by spiritual sacrifice: we have to be willing to surrender some part of ourselves in order to grow. Though it can be frightening, that moment of surrender is often the very instant we begin to change.

And so it became clear to me that my knowledge came at a cost to my innocence: all that pain and fear in my childhood helped to develop the skills I later referred to as my "psychic abilities."

The abusive, violent situation at home made adolescence harder for me than it already was. When I sought out the social worker, I was seeking protection and compassion. When she told me to "Go home like a good girl," something hardened up inside me. My hands gripped each other. As a teenager, I felt everything very deeply and began to seek solace in books about palmistry and intuition. After my visit to Florry Nadall at the Syracuse Hotel, I thought more and more about the future. My fingers eventually began snapping to the beat when I heard music. What had hardened inside me began to soften. Not only did I want a future, but now I could *sense* one—I just did not know how to get there.

I now know that through the interpretation of the shape of the hand and the lines of the palm, we can learn to understand life's possibilities as they are presented or "read" to us. I have learned that becoming familiar with our own possibilities—our proclivities, desires, and innermost goals—is the first step toward uncovering psychic abilities. A simple glimpse at your palm is like discovering a map: it provides a personal path that will lead to a more intuitive and sensitive way of living.

There are as many paths to personal understanding as there are forks in the road on the journey through life. In my own life and through my own experiences, I have found that palmistry—the art of reading the shape, lines, and markings of the palm—is one of the most accessible and certain forms of divination. While I have found palmistry to be the most attainable of the metaphysical practices, I have also learned that acquiring the full knowledge of this practice is far from a simple exercise. Yet, the first step is simple: the study of your hand will begin your journey. As you continue on the path to spiritual and personal understanding, you will gradually come to an acute understanding of this ancient practice through the twelve concepts that unfold in this book.

If you begin by facing your own truths, you will, eventually, find yourself transforming your desires and goals. You will experience, as I did many years ago, an unprecedented realization of consciousness and spiritual connection to others, and finally, you will realize the destiny you hold within. Just as each fingerprint is different, no two hands are exactly alike, and you will come to learn that your hand contains the secrets of your very unique and individual fate.

When I first meet a client, I, like Florry Nadall, take hold of that person's hand. I explain that his or her hand is a spiritual road map that will reveal deeply rooted dreams, hidden feelings, the past, present, and possible future. And through the course of this book, I will reveal the same to you. Experience has shown me that if we can be in the moment, aware of ourselves and our present situation and surroundings, then we will know the future. And the future will take care of itself, moment by moment. But, first, being in the moment requires one essential element: consciousness. For intuition is no more than being fully conscious.

Intuition requires that we trust our instincts. It also demands an awareness of oneself as a thinking being, knowing what one is doing and why; in other words, it means *being present*. And being present requires us to be fully aware of our senses, hearing, seeing, smelling, experiencing whatever is in that moment. If raindrops are falling, being conscious is simply feeling the dampness of those drops against your skin, rather than wishing for a sunny day. It is seeing what is before you without judgment or criticism. Because only without censure can we be present. And once we are present and accounted for, once we are completely conscious, something magical happens, and everything that is theoretically possible becomes realistically probable.

So when we spend our lives searching for possibilities, how do we become conscious? The answer lies in the palm of your own hand.

Searching for my own possibilities during adolescence, I embarked on a solitary study of palmistry. When I was seventeen years old, a local couple, who knew of my family troubles, offered to rent a room recently vacated by their college-bound son to me for fifteen dollars a week. I was in my senior year of high school and I attended classes from seven-thirty A.M. until just before noon. Then, I rushed to work at the General Electric plant from noon until eight P.M., assembling transistor radios. The job was not exciting, but it paid seven dollars an hour, great money in the late sixties, and that excited me. Many of the other employees were college students, and during dinner break they would study calculus and microbiology while I studied palmistry and numerology. The work itself required considerable manual dexterity, so all of us were aware of our hands. When my coworkers heard about my interest in palmistry, many of them asked me to read their palms. So began my first practical study of the human hand.

That year, I read hundreds of palms. I supplemented this "hands-on" application of knowledge by reading everything about the subject that I could. The small bedroom I rented was soon transformed into a library of palmistry and other metaphysical books. As time passed, books on acting and the theater, my other interest, completed my library. When I graduated school, I had saved enough money to purchase a 1954 Chevy convertible, for one hundred dollars, and headed to New York City.

The late sixties were an exciting time to be in the city, especially for a country girl from upstate New York. As soon as I arrived, I tracked down Susan Hoffman, an older friend who had left town before me, who now called herself Viva. Well, Viva had become a *Vogue* model and was a good friend of Andy Warhol's. She introduced me to Andy and to several people in the underground film community. Andy offered me a role in one of his movies—the part of an innocent country girl. I declined, however, because I did not want to take my clothes off on film. Within three months, I did get my first movie role, as an extra on *Midnight Cowboy*. Here I was, eighteen years old and a movie star—well, almost.

I continued to study palmistry and read palms as I worked odd jobs and took acting lessons. Though I was committed to the art of palm reading itself, I also relied on my growing skills for social reasons. Because I was basically a shy person, reading palms was a good way to meet people. And so I found my way in the big city for a few years. For my twentieth birthday, after reading thousands of palms, I decided to treat myself and see one of New York's best known psychics, Vincent Ragone.

He was a soft-spoken, gentle man in his thirties whose loudly colored clothes expressed more about the time period, the end of the psychedelic sixties, than about his nature. He practically whispered that I had been abandoned and killed by my own father in several other lifetimes, and that I was not going to allow myself to be victimized in this lifetime. When I heard that, I nearly fell off my chair. Though I felt I was too young to be facing such a harsh reality, I embraced it, determined to live my life as I chose to.

Vincent also told me that I would be a writer. "But I can't even spell!" I protested. He told me not to worry—that by the time I wrote my book, people would understand me perfectly. Of course, I had no idea what he meant by that. And when he told me that I would be in demand, I was thrilled, because my greatest dream was to become an actress. "Not as an actress," he said, "but as a teacher."

A teacher? I was crushed. All I cared about at the time was my love life, my weight, and fame. Sometimes it was my weight, my love life, and fame—the priorities slightly juggled— but I was too concerned with my own desires at the time to imagine helping others.

And as I write this, I still worry about my spelling. But I am no longer devastated at the thought of being a teacher. Now, my greatest wish is that my lifetime of psychic experience might, indeed, teach others the precious gift of *intuition*.

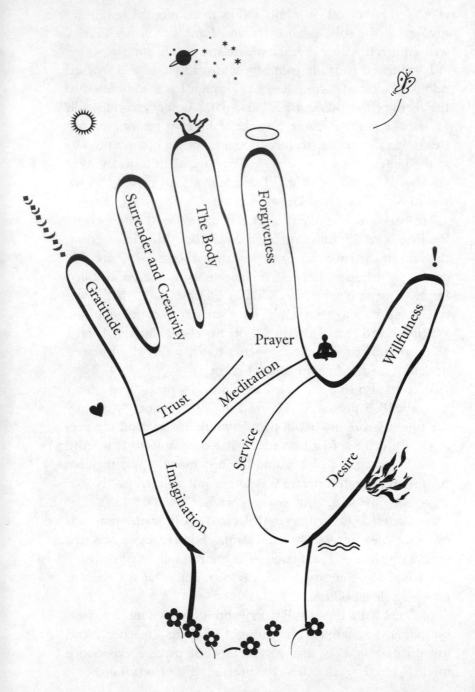

O N E

Palmistry and Intuitive
Perception: A Brief History

As we enter the new millennium, we possess a far more comprehensive understanding of the special relationship between the hand and the mind than ever before. In fact, what was intuitively understood in ancient times has only recently been studied and appreciated by science. The latest revelations in embryology have been remarkable in that they have shown that at the start of the second trimester of pregnancy, the cerebral cortex, the layer of the brain that is the seat of nerve activity, and the distal upper limbs, or hands, begin their development simultaneously. Scientists have concluded that both the cerebral cortex and the hand develop from the same stem cell material—the ectoderm of the fertilized egg cell—which underscores the profound and real connection between the hand and brain.

If we had any doubts before now, we can wholeheartedly embrace what palmists have always understood, that our hand and brain are intimately connected, because at an early point in our development they were one and the same.

Consequently, that there is a constant flow of information between these two essential aspects of ourselves is expected; as with any dynamic interaction, the concept of *change* is part of its very nature. The changes that we experience as our lives unfold are literally manifest in the lines, mounts, and other markings of the palm. Studied together with the size and shape of an individual's fingers, a unique and instructive self-portrait emerges, and we literally hold a map of our unique fate in hand. By learning to read and understand this map, which was formed by our most essential cells early in our development, we can change our lives.

As we know, hands have fascinated humans since prehistoric times. In some cultures, it was believed that hands were magically endowed. Indeed, it seems unlikely that anyone would argue this idea when the proof of that endowment has been displayed and witnessed in countless cultures throughout the centuries. Not only is man capable of making tools and weapons, which give us power over nature and the ability to engage in war, we are also able to make signs and symbols that allow us to share our ideas with each other. Perhaps even more magically, our hands have provided us the means to create and practice poetry, music, science, and art.

So when did the art of palmistry begin?

Considered the earliest art form, the Paleolithic hand imprints found daubed against cave walls in natural mineral pigments such as yellow and red ochre, manganese and iron oxide, combined with charcoal and blood, are a bold testament to the longstanding significance of the human hand to mankind. In even these earliest works, man chose to see the human hand as a reflection of himself and use it as an assertion of his existence. Given this, we can easily grasp that our early ancestors saw the human body as comprised of five points, the head and four limbs, which corresponded to the five points of the hand, the thumb and fingers. In looking at his hand, early man saw himself and came to believe that the life force, the very energy of being, that flowed through him entered through the fingertips and found expression in the various mounts and planes of the palm.

And that is how palmistry began.

When Aristotle, in the fourth century B.C., made mention of palmistry, the practice had, in fact, already existed for thousands of years (it is even mentioned in the Old Testament). The meanings of the lines of the human hand had been deciphered, and palm readings had already foretold innumerable events the world over, most especially in regard to war. The Roman emperor Augustus, and Julius Caesar himself reportedly studied palmistry. Both Caesar and Alexander the Great are believed to have employed the science of hand analysis before battles. Pythagoras, the Greek philosopher (perhaps better known for his mathematical theorem but a student of palmistry, nonetheless), documented the arrival of palmistry in the Western world from the East as early as 582 B.C. The Druids, who were Celtic priests, in the third century B.C., and who were written about by Caesar following their meeting in battle, reportedly believed the hand to be an oracle.

Palmistry reportedly appeared in western Europe in the twelfth century A.D., a period of influx of Arabic knowledge into a part of the world that was just emerging from the so-called Dark Ages. It is difficult to know how and where palmistry may have been practiced in Europe during the Dark Ages because it was a period in which only sanctioned Christian religious knowledge and writing persisted. In contrast, the Moors had preserved the knowledge amassed by the Greek and Roman classic civilizations. During the Moorish conquest and occupation of Spain, this Greek and Roman knowledge, including information on palmistry, was introduced to the Spaniards, surfacing at universities in Cordoba, Toledo, and Seville, and then spread through Europe. French and Spanish translations of Arabic manuscripts, dating back to the twelfth century, include brief notes on palmistry, and the study had certainly spread north because the *Digby Role IV*, the oldest known manuscript focusing on palmistry, was written on vellum in Middle English around 1440. Its main point of discussion focused on the amount of space between the *heart* and *head* lines of the human hand; a narrow expanse between the two lines supposedly suggested stinginess, while a broader space suggested kindness and friendliness.

By the fifteenth century, palmistry had Western followers from all walks of life, scholars and gypsies alike, who began to spread the art throughout Europe, gaining recognition as fortune-tellers. In fact, since it was associated with the noble arts of astronomy and medicine, and with such luminary thinkers as Aristotle and Pythagoras, palmistry was not considered a "demonic" practice (though skills such as midwifery and herb gathering were), and it was granted a true legitimacy even in those close-minded times.

Doctor Johann Faust, legend tells us, was an astrologer and conjurer who roamed Germany in the first half of the sixteenth century and whose dark reputation spawned many books and operas. One of the stories of Faust tells us that he would read palms in exchange for food and drink. It is said that he believed that the future could be beheld in a human hand. As early as 1615, the Rosicrucians, an international organization committed to developing mankind's highest potential and psychic powers, embraced palmistry as a means of self-revelation and published their credo, which found its way to the United States before 1700.

In 1768, Marie-Anne le Normand was born in France and later became a proficient palmist and Napoleon Bonaparte's fortune-teller. Fred Gettings's *The Book of the Hand* informs us that after the siege of Toulon, when Napoleon was merely a successful general, le Normand prophesied that he would "go off to make war in Italy, and return in such glory that you will be the most famous of all Frenchmen." This was indeed the case, as was her warning that Bonaparte should "beware of pride, for it can carry you high, and it can also throw you lower down than you were originally."

In the mid 1800s, Helena Petrovna Blavatsky, a woman of significant psychic faculties, founded the Theosophical Society in order to introduce Eastern ideas into Victorian age philosophies. And as the nineteenth century progressed, two important works surfaced that pointed out the connections between palmistry and contemporary scientific and medical research. *The Psychonomy of the Hand* and *Mysteres de la Main* were written by two Frenchmen, Casimir Stanislaus D'Arpentigny and Adrien Adolphe Desbarrolles, respectively. These two men are considered by some to be the founders of modern palmistry. D'Arpentigny studied hand types and their relationship to various character traits, while Desbarrolles argued that the human palm is at the center of an instinctive life. Desbarrolles believed both past and future illnesses could be seen in the hands, because the nervous system, which controls the body's impulses, ultimately finds form in the mounts and lines of the palm. He also concluded that the apparent future as seen in our hands is not immutable; because we each have our own free will, we hold the possibility of changing our fate, and therefore changing the lines and markings on our hands.

A compellingly modern idea, and yet it is a century old.

By the late nineteenth century, schools of palmistry, or cheirology as they are known in England, were being recognized. Cheirology is the study of the form of the hand and its link to the individual's character and psychological disposition. Katherine St. Hill founded the Cheirological Society in London in the late 1880s with the goal of introducing scientific research standards into the field of palmistry. She hoped to promote the study of palmistry and establish some professional ethics for those practicing the art. She and the Cheirological Society made a significant impact on modern palmistry until the early 1940s, when the torch was taken up by Noel Iaquin and Beryl

Hutchinson when they founded the Society for the Study of Physiological Patterns. This society was aimed at studying a number of established methods, palmistry among them, and discovering new methods to advance the understanding of human nature.

In the United States, palmistry was explained and expounded upon in the early part of the twentieth century in William Benham's comprehensive *The Laws of Scientific Palmistry*. This work, originally published in 1901, is still referenced and studied by palmists today. The connections between the character or temperament of a person and his hands, established as the "psychology of the hand" by the Polish psychologist Charlotte Wolff, gained international attention in the 1940s and 1950s. At a time when metrics, such as the Binet intelligence test, were being developed and widely accepted as methods of evaluating intangible human characteristics, Wolff defended palmistry as a means of evaluating human personality. Her methods were scrutinized by psychologists of the period who asked her to use them in a blind test to diagnose individuals suffering from certain forms of mental illness. The published results of this blind test corresponded closely to the psychologists' own diagnoses. Wolff's work is evidence of the close and ongoing relationship between palmistry and psychology.

The postwar and cold war era heralded in a time of hope and belief in technology and the scientific method. In the U.S., we came to believe that the way to better health, to happiness, and even to the stars lay in "hard science." Consequently, pursuits of less empirical methods of learning and knowing were discredited by our teaching institutions and our popular culture during the late fifties and sixties. Then, a "new age" movement began. It was a time when many paradigms were challenged by the younger members of society. I think now of the Vietnam War, when there was heavy experimentation with hallucinogens and other mind-altering substances and Eastern religions, such as Buddhism and Zen, were introduced to the mainstream. As a result, a more "holistic" approach to life evolved, which acknowledged the link between the physical, spiritual, and emotional realms. As we know, this holistic approach has slowly and steadily gained acceptance and popularity, and we are enjoying a new awareness and appreciation of intuitive abilities.

Today, we live in a period called the information age. While we experience the birth of the "information superhighway"— a term used to refer to the incredible electronic network that is presently combining cable television, telephone, and computer systems, which will ultimately enable most communication to travel the planet at the speed of light—words like "bandwidth," "fiber optic," and "digital" have become part of our daily language. Although at this point nobody knows what final form the "superhighway" will take, experts agree that it will have a dramatic effect on the human race. It will radically transform not only how we communicate, but it will change how we live, learn, and work.

Accompanying this technological revolution, we are also experiencing a revolution within. As the paradigms of culture transform, so too do our personal paradigms and frames of reference. In the industrial age, the machine was the point of reference for everything, including the human body. As a result, we looked at the body in mechanistic terms for many years, only partially understanding its great complexity.

With the advent of the modern age, we began to focus on a new understanding of energy and physics that far surpassed our mechanistic notions, and we have subsequently come to comprehend the human body as a miraculously complex, dynamic, and holistic creation. We are learning that the body is constantly monitoring and interacting with itself and its environment, even at the intracellular level. People no longer talk about the "ghost" in the machine, but about the human

body as a "river of information and energy." While I appreciate the change in focus and value the ideological shift that
accompanies it, I am also deeply aware that the practice of
palmistry and psychic awareness has always provided this very
same understanding. That is why palmistry is more essential
and relevant today than it has ever been.

Today, much of the world's population has become edu-
cated in how we might counteract or, in some cases, merely
survive catastrophes, either man-made or those that we perceive as wrought by God. As a result, we have begun to
embrace and understand the idea that we are responsible for
our own behavior. To that end, we have invented tools to
examine our behavior. We have tried to determine what con-
stitutes good character and to identify humanitarian ideals.
And by questioning our responsibility to our world, we have
begun a momentous dialogue, fueled by questions regarding
free will. What are our true choices about how to live our
lives? What is the effect of family or the environment on our
choices? How might we overcome hurdles and unfortunate
circumstances? What specific problems in our world can we
do something about? How can we get support in responding
to this problematic, complex world? What are our deepest
desires, fears, doubts?

If only we knew the future, we think, we could find the
answers to all our questions and we could make only the right
decisions about how to live our lives. But if we focused only
on the future, we would never get to know ourselves now.
Learning our own personal truths is a lifelong endeavor that
must begin in the present moment. We must learn to trust
our psychic perception, our intuition, to live as honestly as
possible. If we accept this challenge, we can face our flaws,
weaknesses, and limitations, and thereby begin to know and
honor our strengths, uniqueness, and true humanity. And that
is when it will become truly possible for us to shape our world
and our future, and finally discover the meaning of this life.

• • •

Quite often, as I guide people in their personal searches for their deeper individual humanity, I am asked what an *intuitive* is exactly, and what *fate, destiny,* and *psychic perception* are. Far from the negative images of gnarly old fortune-tellers who pored over tattered decks of tarot cards or today's storefront readers who prey on people's fears and doubts, an *intuitive* is someone who possesses highly developed intuitive abilities, abilities that we *all* have to one degree or another. Those, like myself, who practice intuition professionally have chosen to use their skills to grapple with the uncertainty and difficulties that make up life. That is certainly a far cry from entertaining audiences with bogus displays of mind reading and conjuring up false apparitions from the dead.

Many of us have erroneously learned that *fate* is something beyond our control, something that happens *to* you. *Destiny* is supposedly something that you *choose* to realize, such as your potential, something you may actually influence. But the fact is, our individual fate and destiny are both up to us. It is we who decide what our fate will be. If you choose never to leave your house, for example, you will simply live a life in which you do not leave your house. Fate is about choice, and your fate, as this book will illustrate, exists in your very hands.

Psychic perception, then, is a state of heightened intuition. It may be useful to delve a little deeper into this idea, beginning with a discussion of what the psyche itself actually is. In Greek mythology, Psyche was a beautiful nymph, so beautiful, in fact, that the goddess Venus envied and despised her and ordered Cupid (Venus' son) to force her to fall in love with the most contemptible man possible. But Cupid himself fell in love with Psyche, who is considered to be the personification of the soul, and could not comply with Venus' order. After much persecution by Venus, Cupid's love for Psyche and his wish for reconciliation won out, and Psyche was granted immortality. In simplest terms, the *psyche* can be defined as the soul or the mind, not just the thinking brain, but the mind that permeates and connects the disparate aspects of each and every human. The unconscious and sub-conscious, finally, are part of the psyche, and intuition derives from this part of the mind.

According to psychoanalyst Carl Jung, "Intuition . . . is one of the basic functions of the psyche, namely *perception of the possibilities inherent in a situation.*" Our intuition is constantly in play, making judgments, but usually only the outcome, the final judgment made by our intuition, finds its way from the subconscious to the conscious. Psychic perception is a means of tapping into this judgment process, what Charlotte Wolff describes as "the instantaneous synthesis below the level of consciousness of observed details." More important, it involves trusting the process.

If you doubt the existence or power of intuition, simply think of the tortoises that know to return to their birth beaches, the fawns that are born knowing how to run, and the swallows who return each year to Capistrano. If these other species can perform these seemingly miraculous feats simply by being, why is it so hard to accept that humans, too, can *know* through intuition, that they can know simply by being human?

My experience has shown me that trusting this intuition—or finding your psychic self—is the way to control both your fate and your destiny. How many times, for example, have you simply "known" that someone was going to call just as the phone rang? Or had a "hunch" about something that proved to be correct? Many psychologists believe that *déjà vu,* the feeling of having been in a particular situation before despite knowledge to the contrary, is a type of psychic phe-nomenon.

What is known as "psychic phenomena" does not merely represent a sixth sense, however, but ranges from simple intu-ition to extreme states of mystical awareness. When you have a gut feeling about something or go with a hunch, you are doing the same thing a psychic does when she engages in a reading.

But so many of us don't yet trust our gut feelings, which is why I have written, and why you have chosen to read, this book. I have chosen to frame the chapters around the age-old analysis of the hand, for the road map to self-knowledge that it has provided over the centuries is undeniable. And, significantly, the hand is a wonderful *visual aid* that you have access to all the time.

I have witnessed palmistry regain its appropriate status as a tool for self-evaluation. Relied upon in spiritual arenas to provide insight and foresight, it is now also increasingly used in many fields of alternative medicine as a diagnostic tool. Palmistry as a vehicle for increased intuitive awareness is finally gaining credibility and is ascending as a viable and effective means of gaining true self-knowledge. I invite you, then, to trust yourself and to embark on this journey of self-exploration and join me in finding out what fate and life has in store for each and every one of us. Remember, your fate truly is in your hands.

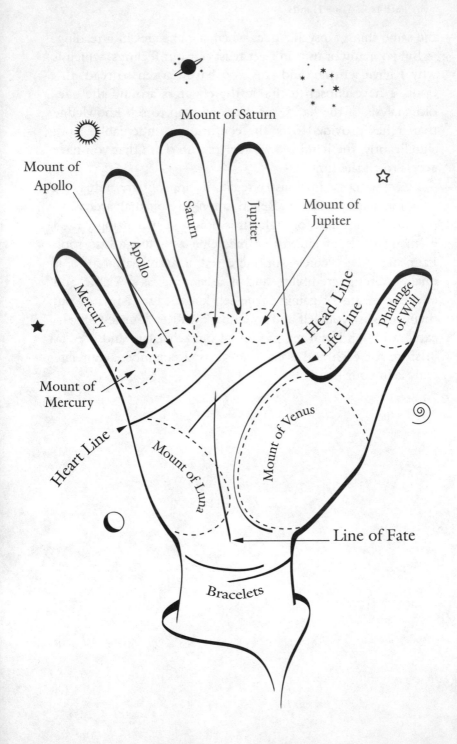

Mount of Saturn

Mount of
Apollo

Saturn

Jupiter

Mount of
Jupiter

Apollo

Mercury

Head Line

Life Line

Phalange
of Will

Mount of
Mercury

Mount of Venus

Heart Line

Mount of Luna

Line of Fate

Bracelets

Your Hand: A Basic Introduction

Because we live in a society in which we shake hands with each other when we meet, I always notice the *size* and *texture* of a person's hands before most anything else. In palmistry, of course, the size and texture of each hand is extremely significant. While I find the specific meaning of each characteristic is only applicable in relation to other aspects of the hand, some universalities can be broadly stated. *Small* hands, then, belong to a sensitive and lively nature, people with *big* plans. *Large* hands, paradoxically, are found on those individuals who often focus on the *small* details in life.

Soft hands are often a sign of a soft heart, belonging to an emotional person, not surprisingly. *Very* soft hands, however, may mean you are something of a pushover; giving in to stress more easily than others; learning to say no will be beneficial for you. *Firm* hands reveal an energetic, active personality.

Taking the *texture* of someone's hands into consideration is also essential when attempting to distinguish particular char-

23

acteristics of personality. To do so, consider the back of the hand. Like sandpaper, there are three distinct skin textures: *fine, medium,* and *coarse.* A *fine* hand is smooth to the touch, more closely resembling porcelain than the remaining two. Its bearer is usually more sensitive or emotional in nature than the others, ready to escape worry and confrontation by intellectual pursuit. A *coarse* hand, distinguished by a rougher texture made apparent by large pores and more hair than the other types, is often found on people with great stamina and staying power. These individuals appreciate the outdoors more than the other types, and tend to express their vitality or anxiety through physical action. A *medium* hand, distinguished by a lesser softness and some visible pores, belongs to an individual whose personality encompasses various elements of the other two. These individuals have good staying power and can handle stress without going too far inward or outward, as the soft or coarse types may.

In addition to the shape and texture of your hands, the other characteristics of the hand—the *lines* and *markings* on your palm, the length and distinguishing characteristics of your fingers—reveal incredible details about who you are. We are all born with three basic lines: the *heart* line, the *life* line, and the *head* line. These lines are the only parts of your hand that will not change significantly over the course of your life. The other lines, certain markings and features of your palm and fingers, will change—perhaps minimally, perhaps dramatically—as your life unfolds.

More than any others, the *heart, life,* and *head* lines reveal the major energies and talents that each of us possess. If we think of these lines as rivers, they can show us what course our life can take. And like rivers, the lines can sometimes *change* their course, but they do start and end somewhere.

The *heart* line begins on the *outside* of the hand, while the *head* and *life* lines begin on the *inside* of the palm. Each of these lines has a beginning and end point, indicating the passage of time.

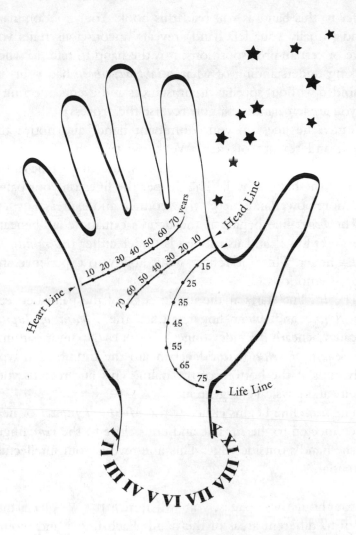

Look at your own hands now and locate these three lines. The first thing you may notice is that they differ on each hand. This is natural, for each hand is presenting us with particular information. Your dominant hand (the hand you write with) charts your life *as you live it,* tending to display your desires and accomplishments and illustrating attitudes and events from the past, present, and future—information that is yours to *become consciously aware of* as we study the hand.

Refer to this hand as you read this book. Your nondominant hand (usually your left hand) reveals unconscious traits you have or certain predispositions; it is the hand to refer to when seeking understanding of what *might have been* had your life unfolded without specific circumstances and events affecting it (if you are left-handed, simply reverse the process).

Study the lines on your dominant hand, and notice the depth and texture of each. We know that the deeper and wider a river is, the more powerful it is, and this is true of the lines of the hand as well. The deeper the lines on your palm, the more power and energy they contain and express.

The *heart* line begins at the hand's outside edge beneath the *pinky* finger and usually ends under either the *middle* or *index* finger. This line reflects your ability to experience and express emotions.

The *life* line starts at the inside edge of the palm between the *thumb* and *index* finger, under the *Mount of Jupiter* (located beneath the index finger). It slopes downward around the *Mount of Venus* (the ridge beneath the thumb) and typically ends at the bottom of the palm. This line records your vitality and physical energy in life.

The *head* line begins either at the *Mount of Jupiter* or near or connected to the *life* line and ends close to the *ring* finger or the hand's outside edge. This line reveals your intellectual potential.

Throughout these pages, you will notice the various names given to different areas of the hand. Each finger and mount of the hand is named after a god or goddess from ancient times, for this is how our ancestors developed an understanding of the world around them. Attempting to come to terms with the mysterious forces of the universe, the ancient Greeks and Romans believed that gods and goddesses could control the fate of mortals. The great power and authority each god supposedly possessed was thought to preside over all of creation; authority was divided among the gods so that each of them had power over a specific aspect of life. But for all their power, the gods experienced emotions, such as love, pride, and jealousy, which made them seem approachable to human beings. If you were dissatisfied with a certain aspect of your life, you prayed or made an appropriate sacrifice, hopeful that your request would be honored by the god who had control over that specific area.

Over the years, many cultures held on to the belief of the powers of the gods. Gradually, people began to believe that gods and goddesses represented universal forces that flowed through everyone, that love, creativity, intellect, ambition, imagination, desire, and power were part of *everyone's* divine makeup. As more time has passed, we have come to realize that our fate is not controlled by powerful forces *outside* of us, but by the forces that exist *inside* of us. And we can detect the presence of these forces by observing our hands.

In these pages, you will also read various explanations regarding the different markings that appear on your hand. While a particular marking may mean the same thing on various areas of the palm, quite often the meaning of a marking is specific to the area on which it appears. For example, a *star* on the *Mount of Venus* may mean increased possibilities for love or a wonderful surprise in your life. A *star* on the *Jupiter* (or *index*) finger may mean good, even great, fortune. You will be able to distinguish these differences as you read through each chapter, where the particular meanings are specified and explained.

As you begin to study the lines and markings of your hand, you will notice that they begin to change as your thought patterns change. The exercises at the end of each chapter will help you make these changes and move toward greater self-fulfillment.

Think of your hand as a spiritual road map that was created solely to guide you along the road of life. The journey you choose to undertake as you read the following chapters and complete each chapter's exercises promises a combination of knowledge, clarity, and spirituality, which taken together, will lead you toward realizing your intuitive abilities. Self-knowledge (a lifelong pursuit) is a wondrous and powerful experience. Yet, it occurs only after the brambles of confusion have been cleared from its path. Each chapter, then, will lead you beyond confusion to clarity. Spirituality, a natural partner to clarity, will surely follow. Finally, the convergence of knowledge, clarity, and spirituality will guide you to the highest summit: your intuitive self.

And so, with our hands to guide us, we now challenge the darkness of our unknown selves. The more we understand the map of our lives, the easier it becomes to find meaning and the light of self-knowledge. Following are some basic illustrations that show the *basic* meaning of the aspects of the

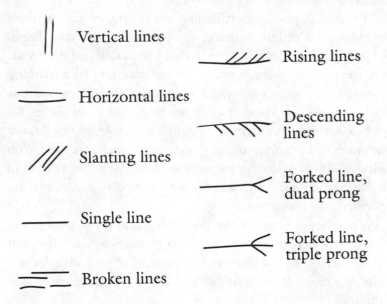

The Lines of the Hand

palm; more *specific* definitions for these aspects of the hand
will appear later in the book.

Here are the particular lines and markings that can be
found, in truly unique and specific formations, on every
hand.

Lines

Deep lines are a sign of energy, physical strength, vitality, and
endurance. A deep *heart* line suggests a good, fair nature,
capable of generosity, true friendship, and inner serenity. A
deep *life* line indicates the tendency to find the right solu-
tions to problems as they arise. A deep *head* line reveals a
warm nature and well-developed intellect.

Pale, shallow, or light lines are a sign of weaker energy and
possibly sickly physical constitution, likely found on those
who exhibit a tendency to worry. A pale *heart* line indicates a
tendency toward sentimentality, though it may be balanced
by a tranquil nature. A pale *life* line represents a passionate,
receptive nature, capable of asserting itself, even argumenta-
tively. A pale *head* line is found on a sensitive person who
usually needs more sleep than average to recover from the
impact of daily, waking life.

Clear, simple lines are often found on serene, well-balanced
individuals, whereas **Broken** lines may indicate an incon-
stancy or inability to see things through; they may also reveal
a change in location or direction of life itself. These lines do
not signal bad health unless there are corroborative markings
(such as *chains*). A break on the *heart* line may signal the end
of an affair, an emotional trauma, a change of events, or even
an illness. A break on the *life* line indicates that attention to
good health is required. A break on the *head* line reveals a
desire for self-improvement.

Long lines are found on individuals with a wide range of interests and who are apt to speculate. Long *heart* lines indicate unselfish natures regarding love, likely belonging to those with good, fair natures. Long *life* lines suggest a constitution of good balance, providing physical and intellectual strength. Long *head* lines represent those with a range of intellectual interests, capable of mental and emotional flexibility.

Short lines indicate intensity and often a personality that is constantly trying to define love through loved ones. Short *heart* lines indicate shortened affections. Short *life* lines indicate possible good health coupled by a shortened life (though that is *not always* the case. It is important to remember that the markings on the *entire* hand have more to do with the length of someone's life than this line alone). Short *head* lines indicate a mind prone to focus on mundane affairs.

Wavy lines suggest a mind that is easily distracted, found on individuals who may find it difficult to pay attention for long periods. A wavy *heart* line reveals a personality apt to experience occasional adventures or brief flirtations. A wavy *head* line indicates imagination and creative ability.

Curving lines represent creativity. Curving *heart* lines represent an extroverted personality, able to express feeling spontaneously. A curving *head* line can be found on the palms of many writers and artists. A curving *life* line is natural.

Straight lines indicate "straight" personalities, those who stay on course, displaying a practical outlook, especially in the case of straight *life* lines. Straight *heart* lines indicate a personality likely to reserve or contain emotion, especially in relation to love. A straight *head* line reveals a realistic, analytic mind.

Slanting lines suggest a strong personality, found on those who may act in an authoritative or advisory capacity.

Vertical lines are found on those with a strong desire to cooperate with or to please others.

Horizontal lines may be short or long. Short horizontal lines indicate obstacles regarding the free flow of energy. Longer horizontal lines reveal an exposure of privacy or conflict. These lines may also indicate signs of separation from loved ones or marriage partners if located on the *Mount of Venus* and can indicate marriage or significant relationships if found beneath the *Mercury* (or *pinky*) finger.

Double lines, also known as sister lines, appear as parallel lines reinforcing the characteristics of the given line beside which they appear. A double *heart* line is a sign of great physical strength and also indicative of a character capable of providing well. A double *life* line reveals a *guardian angel,* most likely a loved one who has passed over, who is watching over you. A double *head* line is a sign that a person has two careers or two main intellectual interests in life.

Forked lines appear at the end of a line that splits. Forks may indicate a decrease in energy or reveal balance and adaptability, depending on where they are found. A fork at the end of a *heart* line indicates a split in emotions concerning love and a tendency to be cautious. A fork on the *head* line reveals a character prone to exaggeration. A *double-pronged* fork increases the potential for self-expression. A *triple-pronged* fork usually indicates intense emotional power, and indicates genius. This type of line is usually found on a person capable of handling three careers or areas of interest (such as family, career, and hobby) or can be manifest as being scatterbrained (like the absent-minded professor).

Other Markings

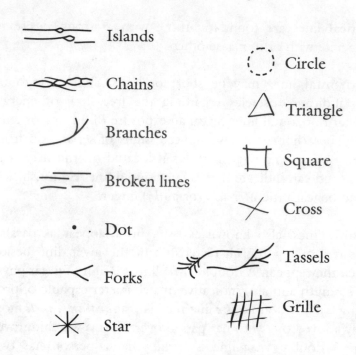

Islands

Chains

Branches

Broken lines

Dot

Forks

Star

Circle

Triangle

Square

Cross

Tassels

Grille

Islands hinder the strength of any line in your hand, indicating loss, trouble, or illness. Islands on the *heart* line suggest that depression or fear is the emotional state. Islands on the *life* line can mean that there is a tendency toward ill health, a physical weakness, or depression. Islands on the *head* line may indicate troubled concentration or psychological difficulties.

Chains indicate a very emotional person, prone to ill health as a result of worry. This individual exhibits a tendency toward drama or turmoil and, depending on their placement on the hand, may experience periods of vacillation, scattered energy, or confusion. Chains on the *heart* line reveal an emotionally sensitive person, easily wounded by others, who may also long for intimacy while fearing commitment. Chains on the *life* line indicate health issues that need to be addressed, especially if an *island* accompanies its presence. Chains on the *head* line tend to be found on the hands of those who worry over career matters.

Branches may reach in either direction on the palm. *Rising* branch lines are a positive sign, and *descending* lines, which point to the bottom of the hand, point to a decrease in power. Descending branches can indicate disappointment or energy gone awry.

Dots suggest a surprising shock to the body or emotions. Dots on the *heart* line indicate a physical or emotional setback. Dots on the *life* line suggest a period of ill health. Dots on the *head* line reveal a shock of some kind, usually related to career.

Rascettes, which I call *bracelets,* are the lines that appear on the underside of the wrist. Thirty years of good health is attributed to each strong, unbroken line. Chained rascettes suggest a weak physical condition and have been linked to gynecological troubles in women.

Stars are rarely seen. They are omens of great fortune or tragedy. True stars comprise six or more lines and are distinctly formed. They may also suggest wonderful surprises or an increase of love and passion, depending on where they are located.

Circles are seldom seen. They are believed to signify fame in the bearer's life and can be found beneath the *Saturn* (or *middle*) finger. Though I have read the palms of many "famous" people, I have not seen *one* circle in this area.

Triangles indicate an aptitude for serious studies or a gift for the supernatural. Likely to be short-lived wherever they appear, triangles are welcome signs.

Squares, sometimes called *teacher squares,* appear on the palms of individuals so secure in their knowledge they can share it easily. Depending on where they are found, they may also signify an increased protection from possible danger.

Crosses may indicate emotional setbacks or potential. Crosses on the *heart* line suggest blocks in expressing affection. Crosses on the *life* line, often called the Saint Andrew cross, may indicate a potential to save someone's life. Crosses on the *head* line indicate imagined obstacles.

Tassels are rarely seen, but indicate a breakdown or scattering of energy or ability relating to the lines they appear on.

Grilles are cross-hatched lines. Their placement on the palm intensifies the meanings of other markings found at the same location, though they may also imply confusion or obstacles. Generally, the presence of grilles anywhere on the hand is short-lived.

Like snowflakes, no two palm prints are alike. A snowflake, however, does not alter its pattern, while the lines of the palm can *change*. In fact, by the time you have finished reading this book, some of the markings covering your palm will most likely have transformed. Generally speaking, the lines on your hand change every three to six months—or more often if you are one of the few human beings who makes change, rather than habit, a habit.

It is useful, then, to make and keep a copy of our own handprint, for it becomes a map of our existence. This allows us to look back and actually see the changes in ourselves and in certain circumstances of our lives, which undoubtedly, and often almost imperceptibly, find form in our palms.

The easiest way to keep a record of your progress is to make a copy of your hand on a copying machine. If you choose this route, I recommend spending the extra few dollars to use a color copier, where less shadow and more delineation is offered. *Repeat* this procedure every three to six months or when significant events occur in your life.

And now, with an initial grasp of the hand's complexity and promise more clearly in mind, we are prepared to begin the journey to our deepest, intuitive, selves.

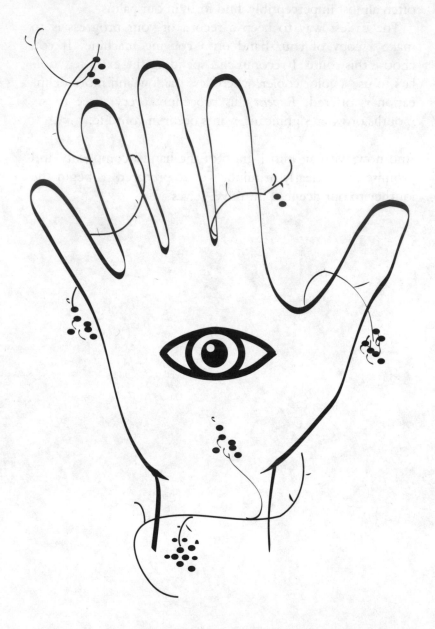

Your Hand Will Reveal Your Truth.

THREE

Truth: Your Intuitive Awareness

Over the past twenty-five years of practicing palmistry and using my intuition, I have learned that each of us longs for a deeper sense of who we really are. Just as there are different fingers and lines on the hand that bring to our attention these deeper aspects of ourselves, there are also different types of intuitive awareness. I have learned that my intuitive ability comes from knowing the truth and that the more truthful I am about my own life the more intuitive I become. The first principle of intuitive awareness that we must find and cultivate, then, is *truth*.

In my experience, there are three main ways that we avoid having a relationship with truth: often, we are aware of something but do not accept or admit it; two, we do not honor and acknowledge our deepest dreams and goals; three, we don't take responsibility for our actions. All three avoidance techniques must be replaced with acceptance if we are to live more truthfully. Many of us, unfortunately, ignore this simple concept. We then wonder why our lives are not what we would like them to be.

37

I help clients become more self-reliant and self-empowered by learning to accept their own truths and to become aware of the talents and abilities they already possess by using the tools of palmistry and intuition. This is possible when people are willing to take responsibility for the situations in which they find themselves, as a result of personal choices or larger societal influences. As the mass culture we live in focuses on the glossy, sophisticated, and superficial, it blocks intuition, making it more difficult for people to look honestly at what kind of individual they really are. In order to become more intuitive and self-reliant, however, each person must uncover and acknowledge his or her own inner truths.

It is not unusual for people to contact me when they are confused or upset about something. Quite often, new clients want to tell me everything about a particular situation or person, and they are very surprised when I ask them to sit quietly and simply open their palms before they disclose anything about their lives.

If clients begin by "telling all," any skepticism they have will interfere with and color the reading. For example, if a woman tells me that her problem is with her husband, and if during the reading I agree, she may convince herself that I am of no use to her. My uninfluenced predictions, however, may surprise her. When clients are silent, I can ascertain more about their mental state. I can see certain aspects of their personality in their palms, and I can sense in their body language just how responsive they will be to the information their reading will reveal.

Part of my responsibility toward a client is to sense just how responsible they will be with the information I give them. As we all know, it is not easy to digest bad news. On the other hand, it can be argued that all information is good. I believe we must learn to acknowledge every aspect of our lives, even the difficult and unfortunate aspects, if we are to transform ourselves.

The truth, in my experience, creates its own path, but it is often a daunting path beset with the brambles and vines of confusion, doubt, fear, and the inability to accept what *is*. Yet, the truth itself is merely what is, and accepting this concept expresses our capacity to *be*. Our simply *being* reveals a belief in ourselves and the process of our lives that we may not even be aware of. Clearing truth's path is the task of the psyche as it struggles to find clarity and, finally, meaning. How can you clear your own path? In many cases, you can do this by accepting what you already know.

Not long ago, a woman named Roberta came to see me. Fifty-five years of age and married, she was extremely upset and wanted to blurt out her situation, and get to the "meat" of the reading in a hurry. I offered her a cup of tea and asked her to sit quietly for a few minutes and simply breathe. After an opening prayer, which is how I begin every reading, I asked to see her palms, and I immediately sensed her problem. Not only was her *thumb pointed* and *narrow*, indicating insecurity, Roberta's *head* and *life* lines were connected at a point nearly an inch from the outside of her hand and were entwined with *chains*. Chains signify stress and anxiety. And because the chains appeared at the junction of these two major lines, they indicated that she had been in a particularly stressful situation for some time. Too, Roberta's hands were *small*, revealing her sensitive nature, *soft*, which let me know she might rely on her imagination more than reason, and *pale*, which meant that materialism was important to her.

I told her that she believed her husband was cheating on her. "Do you see my husband?" she asked, her eyes wide with surprise. In my mind's eye, I certainly did. I described him: dark hair, mustache, bald spot, medium build with a small paunch, five feet ten inches tall. "You've been married about twenty-five years," I said. "Twenty-seven years," she whispered, "I've been married to Roy. What else do you see?"

I described a man with food around him, though not in a restaurant. I saw a woman in a pink cotton jacket as well. She was standing behind a counter, and she, too, was surrounded by food. The woman was younger than Roberta's husband by fourteen years, divorced, with two children.

Roberta interrupted to say that her husband was a butcher and had a grocery store, and that the woman was the cashier.

My real work as an intuitive begins at this moment: it is my job to help empower my client to see *and accept* the truth for herself. Roberta had been unhappily married for many years, and so had Roy. Nevertheless, Roberta blurted out, "I can't believe he could do this to me. I have been faithful to Roy my whole married life!" Crying and upset, Roberta vowed to find her own lover. "I will confront him as soon as I get home!"

After letting Roberta express her feelings of resentment, I made another suggestion. "Try to put the attention on yourself rather than on Roy. If you do, he will come to you in a way that he hasn't in years. This situation could actually be a very good experience for both of you."

The result of the reading was that the reality of the situation, ultimately, did set Roberta free. Facing up to the truth— not that Roy was cheating, but that Roberta had been unhappy for a long time and she needed to see herself and Roy in a different light—was what changed her life.

Soon after Roberta moved into her own apartment, Roy stopped seeing the cashier at the store and started courting Roberta again. Once she was able to forgive him, the two began to communicate with each other honestly—something they had not done for many years. Eventually, Roberta moved back home.

After admitting the truth to herself about the way things really were in her marriage—information Roberta already

possessed, but could not access before coming to see me—
she took a major step toward clearing her path. She was then
able to begin to make changes in her life that ultimately
made her much happier. And happiness is one of the positive
and delightful expressions of truth.

Carrie, a young internist in her late twenties, is another
example of someone who already knew a certain truth about
her life but was unwilling or unable to face it.

When Carrie appeared at my office, her beautiful green eyes
and long black hair did not conceal the tic that appeared
intermittently on one side of her face. Only twice in my career
have I come across someone with such a pronounced twitch.
The first person had told me that the twitch occurred when
she was *lying* about something, which, of course, I considered
once more as Carrie sat down.

Her hand was *small* and *thin* and cold to the touch. In a
resting position, Carrie's *thumb* hid behind her other fingers.
When she spread open her palm, I noticed that her thumb
had a *clubbed tip,* indicating a certain impatience with life and
the tendency to avoid the truth; *chains* covered her *heart*
line; and *islands* marked her *head* line, most especially at the
areas of her palm that indicate the present time. I knew that
before me sat a troubled, unhappy person. While her small
hands revealed a sensitive personality, likely to be strongly
intuitive, the coldness of them expressed the anxious psychic
battle she must have been experiencing. Several *vertical* lines
beneath her *Mercury* (or *pinky*) finger indicated a specific
healing ability. Though I knew that Carrie had come to talk
about her relationship (that "just knowing" part of me had
perceived this), I began the reading by asking Carrie if she
was happy being a doctor.

She looked at me blankly for a moment. "How do you
know I'm a doctor?" she demanded. I pointed out the vertical
lines. "You are a healer," I said. "Why do you want to know?"

she asked nervously; "I came here for another reason." I told Carrie I saw an island marking her head line, which usually lets me know that someone is feeling stuck in a profession, perhaps having outgrown it. That's when Carrie's face began twitching, and it did not stop for the rest of our session.

"I don't want to talk about that now," she stated, and so the reading proceeded to other matters. The *chains* on her *heart* line indicated confusion or difficulty in a love relationship, her ostensible reason for coming to see me. "Carrie," I said, "I feel that you may be getting married in the near future, but your hand shows me that you are not one hundred percent sure about going through with it. Is that so?" Carrie's eye began twitching wildly. "I can't help but notice your eye trouble," I continued. Carrie shrugged. "Oh, it rarely happens"—she hesitated—"only when I am feeling out of control."

I suggested we take a few deep breaths before continuing. After a few moments, I said softly, "Carrie, you have come to me for a psychic reading. My responsibility is to tell each and every client the truth as I see it. To me, the truth is the cornerstone of freedom. In your case, what I sense is this: You truly dislike, even hate, what you are doing as a doctor, and you have enormous anxiety about the man you are planning to marry. I know that you've come here to ask me if the marriage is going to work out and that you are having doubts about this person. As the saying goes, our eyes are the windows to our souls, and yours are twitching. When that happens, your eyelids close. Imagine your eyelids as shutters or blinds on windows: each time you twitch, you no longer see the truth, but you are full of fear and dread. You just said that your eye twitches only when you feel out of control, so can you tell me what is causing this tremendous distress?"

Carrie's thumbs slid back to their hiding place behind her fingers, and she began to sob. She told me that her wedding, which had been planned for over a year, was scheduled for a month from today. Her future husband, also an internist, was "the perfect match," according to her parents, who had introduced them. Carrie went on to confess that she felt he was a nice person but that she had never been in love with him. Finally, she said, it was the words I had just spoken that made her realize how much she disliked her profession. "I don't know how to face it all; I just can't."

Carrie wanted to please her parents, who had sacrificed in order to send her to the best schools so that she could become the doctor in the family. What she really wanted, she confessed, was to work with animals instead of people. She did not want to marry her fiancé, and she wanted to leave her practice.

As she spoke, I watched the tic subside completely. Carrie's unwillingness to express her truth had found form in that nervous twitch. Before she left my office, she became determined to return to the truth of her life: she would reimburse her parents for her education, hold off on this wedding, and get back into school so that she could become the veterinarian she had always wanted to be.

Another kind of truth that we must learn to embrace is the truth about what we really want from life. The following example illustrates this idea perfectly.

Lawrence was a top executive for a Fortune 500 company, but he had lost his job during a corporate takeover a few years before we met. At fifty-seven, he was having a hard time trying to find a similar position.

We met on a Saturday afternoon in Westport, Connecticut, at the request of Lawrence's wife. He was a patrician-looking man in a cashmere sweater, blue blazer, and slacks. I took his hand and saw that it was one of near perfect balance: long fingers and clear lines free of stress, except for the *life* line.

An *island* appeared in the center of the life line, signifying fear or depression. The hand itself was *long,* which usually indicates someone who is cautious and thoughtful, and *thin,* revealing his introverted, even melancholy nature. His *thumb,* though *long,* indicating his ability to accomplish his goals, was as *stiff* as could be, revealing rigidity. I told Lawrence he was very depressed because he was not working—a statement that surprised him, because he had not offered this information. He assumed his wife had told me he was unemployed, but she had not.

I assured him that I had not discussed his emotional state with anyone, including his wife. I told him his career was a big part of his identity and that he felt increasingly depressed and disappointed the longer he could not find work. With tears in his eyes, Lawrence nodded. He said he could not even get a job in a hardware store and that his wife had gone back to work to pay their basic expenses. They were even spending their savings in order to keep their home.

I told him that his current situation was actually a great opportunity to find out what he really wanted to do. I then told him I saw him gardening most of the day, and his eyes lit up and he smiled. "I do love my garden more than anything—when I am not worrying about bills or the future," he said.

I saw that he could be very successful in the gardening field. Doubtful, Lawrence asked, "But how can I support my family?" I suggested that if he really wanted a new career, it was entirely possible for him to redesign his plans and find new ways to meet his financial needs and goals. Why not sell some extra property to seed whatever venture he chose to pursue? It was clear to me that his family would support him and that he would, in fact, bring the family closer together by making this change: they would all be part of the business. I just sensed that Lawrence would be happy surrounded by plants and flowers—growing things!

Lawrence listened intently.

After a few more unhappy attempts to reenter the corporate world, Lawrence started a business in upscale gardening supply. Within a year, he was also a successful landscape design consultant, and several members of his family worked alongside him.

At the end of our session, I had handed Lawrence the audiocassette that had captured our words on tape—a service I perform for every client. After listening to the tape again and again, he later told me, Lawrence was able to hear and ultimately accept his own truth. By mustering the courage to admit what he really wanted out of his life, Lawrence was able to realize his dream.

And that is the remarkable power of the truth.

In all of these examples, it was necessary for my clients to tell themselves the truth about their circumstances, vastly different though they were. And because each person was willing to begin the process of looking within for his or her own particular truths, each one was able to begin the remarkable journey toward developing intuitive skills. An undeveloped psyche is like a forest full of tangled vines: take one misstep and you may trip over an unknown aspect of yourself. By starting to clear their paths, these clients moved one step closer to grasping and realizing the power of intuitive awareness. And that awareness finds physical form in our hands.

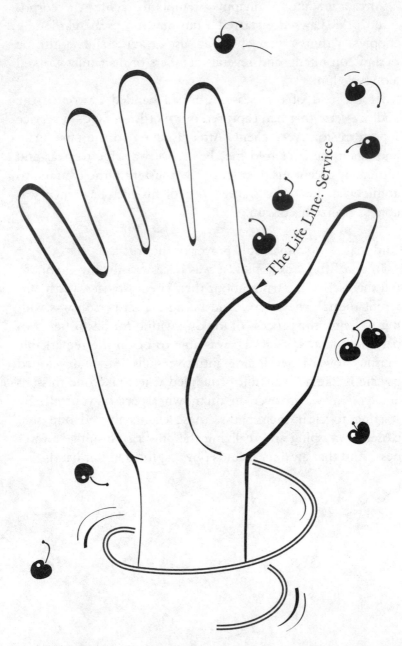

The Life Line: Service

The Life Line Indicates Vitality, Physical Energy, and Service.

FOUR

Service: The Life Line

According to Greek mythology, the thread of life was woven by Clotho, one of the three goddesses of Fate. After Clotho spun this vital thread, her sister Lachesis measured its length, which indicated how long an individual would live. Atropos, the third sister, finally cut the thread, symbolic of life's end. This symbolism is projected onto the palm's *life* line, and it reflects the most frequently asked question I hear from my clients: "How long is my life?" My answer is always the same and always surprises people: "The life line is not meant to reveal *when* we will die, but rather to describe *how* we live."

The life line is, of course, the principal line of the hand. It begins at the edge of the palm between the *thumb* and *index* finger, arcing downward around the *Mount of Venus* toward the center of the wrist, below the *heart* and *head* lines. When significant physical events such as illness, accident, and other forms of trauma touch our lives, they are recorded here. When life changes and we embark on a different course from the one we have been following, that shift also becomes visible. The life line also acts as a *time line* and records information about significant events that have or will take place in our lives. While exact dating is not possible, it is extraordinary to learn that our own hand is a unique timepiece that records the auspicious events of our lives in surprisingly accurate detail.

The life line rarely reveals the actual length of someone's life, as is so widely believed. Instead, it indicates our *vitality* and *physical energy*. Whenever you see a *broken* or *short* life line, therefore, it is important to remember that, as with every aspect of your hand, this will change as you transform your life.

The fact is, no two life lines are the same. You will undoubtedly notice as you study both your dominant and nondominant hand that each line exists in a world of its own: the world of the possible (nondominant hand) and the world of the actual (dominant hand). How we read this information will provide incredibly accurate and insightful information about who we really are.

If your life line is *long, clear,* and *well-defined,* good health and vitality are yours; most likely, you will have a long life and you will meet life's challenges head-on. A *short, clear,* and *well-defined* line indicates good health and a certain intensity, but you may have the tendency to run yourself dry. You may forget to rest and you may be ruled by a sense of adventure and risk taking. If your life line is simply short and not particularly well-defined, it is a sign that your energy, not necessarily your life, is limited.

A *shallow* or *weak* life line reveals a lack of sustained energy, possibly because of a susceptibility to illness or, in some cases, the presence of hypochondriacal tendencies. Similarly, a *long, shallow* life line may indicate a weak constitution and a vulnerability to physical illness, nervousness, and indecision.

When the life line is *connected* to the *head* line, we may identify the age at which that person truly became an individual and separated from their family in an emotionally healthy way. This is exactly when someone truly "leaves home." If the life line and head line are connected late into life, this indicates an unhealthy and ongoing attachment to our family of origin and may signal the tendency to remain too long in an unhealthy marriage or relationship. Not surprisingly, the connectedness of these two lines reveals a careful, cautious character, indicating that the bearer may be apt to linger over decision making. When the life line is *separate* from the head line, conversely, a self-reliant, rather impulsive nature is evident. Taking more time to make decisions would probably benefit the bearer of such lines, since that person is prone to being impatient and even reckless at times.

A feature seen only on the life line is the presence of another line, sometimes called the *sister* or *antibody* line. It is believed by some that you have the gift of recuperation from any illness if you possess a double line, for it signifies that the bearer is doubly protected. I like to think of this second line as the palm's *guardian angel*, for I have witnessed it on the hands of clients who believe that a special one who has passed on is watching over them.

Before I continue a discussion of the various *markings* of the life line, I want to emphasize the importance our own attitudes play in regard to our lives. I have witnessed on the hands of countless clients the proof that *as we change*, so too do the lines on our hands. So rather than read them as any sort of indictment or unchanging pronouncement about who we are or how our lives will unfold, we must remind ourselves that they are merely a reflection of where we are *now* in life and that as we grow and change, so will the markings and characteristics of our hands.

Actual *breaks* in the life line—as opposed to one that *splits*, with a *repair* line behind the break—are indicative of physical trauma. The bigger or deeper the break, the more intense, or lasting, the trauma. In a line that *splits* and is supported by a parallel *repair* line, you can anticipate a change in your life's circumstances. And this can take many forms. With a line that stops halfway down the palm, breaks, and then resumes and travels to the palm's bottom, you can be sure that a physical move awaits you. It may be close at hand or far in the future, and more detailed information about this will be revealed by the other information your hand reveals.

Islands on the life line suggest lapses in health, and depending on placement, they may indicate general physical weakness. If you contemplate the times of illness in your life, you may realize that they were accompanied by periods of indecision.

Chained life lines reveal a very emotional person who may be beset by mental turmoil and periods of confusion. A severely chained life line may be found on the palms of many people whose relationship to fitness and physical activity is only sporadic at best. If you want a long, healthy life, pack this book into your duffel bag now and head over to the gym! If you have a chained life line, you are also the type who experiences physical symptoms as a result of emotional upset.

When *dots* appear on the life line, this may indicate an experience of sudden shock or may signal when in life you have experienced minor health problems.

Branches on the life line, depending on their direction, are hopeful indicators: if your life line begins on or branches *upward* toward the *Mount of Jupiter*, success in your life is promised, for within you resides the optimism, ambition, and drive to overcome any obstacles you may face. If a line branches *downward* and points to the *Mount of Luna* (near the wrist, below the pinky), you most likely have a strong wish to travel, for yours is a restless personality, always wanting to be on the go.

We all possess a *life* line; however, not all of us possess a *fate* line. Also known as the *Saturn* line or the line of *fortune*, the fate line appears on the hands of approximately thirty percent of the population. I have often seen a fate line on the hands of people who view life as a game of chance that they believe they have won. In other words, the fortune line is often apparent on the hands of those who have been *lucky*.

But there is more to the fate line than mere luck, for as these chapters will reveal, our fate lies in our own hands. It is only natural, then, that we actually become capable of *creating* a fate line as the focus in our lives changes from being limited solely to the exigencies of our own existence—often ignoring the care and needs of others—to embracing both the daily and spiritual reality of the larger world around us.

For those of us lucky enough to have understood our own natures early (even preverbally) in life, the fate line may *begin* near the *base of the palm*; more often, it starts mid-palm, representing a significant discovery of self, during adolescence or later. Regardless of its starting point, the fate line crosses the *head* and *heart* lines vertically, extending to the base of the *Saturn* (or *middle*) finger.

The *deepest* fate lines I have seen exist on the hands of those who are impassioned with immense drive and vitality, such as Mother Teresa. In every case, these rare individuals have centered their lives around caring for others and have dedicated themselves to a life of service.

More often, fate lines are *splintered, feathered, frayed,* or *islanded,* revealing the very human tendency to lose focus, miss opportunities, and waste energy. Is there any one of us who has not lost, missed, or wasted an opportunity in our lives?

Teddy's story illustrates the power of fate and the fate line. We met several months ago when Jeanette, the director of the prayer group I belong to, invited him to share his story with us one evening. Jeanette had read an article about Teddy in the local newspaper, and she was so moved by his intentions that she wanted Teddy to share them with us.

And so, Teddy appeared one night to tell his story. He owned a health club up the island, but felt that it was fated that he give up the health club and move to upstate New York to start a camp for teenagers. He didn't want to sell the health club, he explained, he wanted to *give* it to the person who wrote the best essay about why he or she wanted to own a health club and what it would do for his or her own life, as well as the lives of others. To enter this "contest," prospective owners would have to send one hundred dollars; the sum of the lottery would then be the purchase price of the club. The winner of the contest would be chosen by a panel of fair-minded people in the community.

As Teddy related how he had arrived at this idea, I watched as the hearts of a room full of people responded to this man. Ironically, it brought tears to many eyes to hear how just months ago Teddy had wanted to kill his wife because she was leaving him and planned to take their sons to California. At the time, he said, he was a "spiritual mess." The depth of his negativity and depression were apparently so fierce his brother and sister took away all of his hunting guns and began watching over him twenty-four hours a day.

After agonizing for days about the "miserable situation" that Teddy called his life, he said he was able to release his anger and hatred one day. Apparently, instead of killing himself and his wife, he decided that he would "give a gift to God and not hurt either of them," because that would leave his two boys orphans in the world. He started crying and laughing, he said, because he realized that such a "gift" was to *himself,* not to God. His terrible mental condition became clear to him then, and he realized that his all-engulfing anger had been controlling and ruining his life.

"It was a huge turning point for me," he said, "probably the biggest in my entire life. I realized that I could no longer blame anyone in my life for anything and that a tremendous part of my problem was that I had never trusted anyone. At that moment, I took responsibility for everything in my life that I felt victimized by—the misery of my job, my ruined marriage. I called my wife immediately and apologized for one hundred percent of the relationship. I hoped one day she would forgive me. She was a little surprised by my gesture, and that felt good. Then, I turned over the daily operation of my gym to one of my top employees so I could walk the Appalachian Trail."

That was the day, Teddy said, his life changed. He gave most of his belongings away, wrote a will, and planned his Appalachian trip. Now even more concerned, Teddy's brother and sister thought he might simply be planning to kill himself at this juncture, but this was the furthest thing from the truth. "I just needed to get away for a while and walk."

And so he did. He took off his shoes and walked in the woods for over two months. He carried a sleeping bag, tent, poncho, and backpack. The point of the trip was to talk to God and to find out where his life was going and to learn not to look back. On the trails, other hikers, properly clad with sophisticated gear and shoes, looked at Teddy with fear, as if he were crazy. "Maybe I was," Teddy quietly admitted.

One day, at the base of a mountain, the trail he was on came to a fork. "I was about to go left when I heard an agonized cry on the path on my right." He went toward the sound and began to shrug off his backpack, thinking he might need to help someone. Before he could get the pack off his back, however, a bear cub ran across his path. "Fine, I thought, now I've seen a bear," he said, watching the bear cub waddle off and begin to climb a tree.

Just then, he heard another sound to his left—the sound

of breaking branches. He turned and looked directly into the eyes of the cub's mother, a black bear that towered two feet over him. Teddy is a man of six feet, so that was one big bear. "We stared at each other," he said, while the cub waddled back from its romp up the nearby tree.

"I didn't budge, and Mama bear finally walked away," Teddy explained. "Then her baby decides to sit down at my feet like a puppy. I'm afraid to pick up the cub, worried that my scent would cause its mother to reject it or something." So Teddy stood still as the cub walked around him, tugging on his pant legs and rubbing its rump against him. Finally the cub wandered off to climb a tree.

Teddy began to walk away and soon found himself crying. He said he realized that his desire to protect the cub symbolized his tender feelings for his own sons, and it became clear to him that fighting their mother for custody would not be best for them or for their mother. Still crying, he began to pray that God would help him find his own path and show him what he should do with his life.

"Suddenly, it came to me," Teddy explained. "I should start a camp for kids who do not have anyone. Lost, angry teens like I was, and still am. Walking along, trying to walk out my anger and my fear, I knew I needed to start a camp for teens." Directly after this, the idea about giving away his health club followed.

At the prayer group that night, Teddy read us a few of the essays he had so far received. They were remarkably sweet and sometimes deeply touching. Everyone who met Teddy that night at the group was so impressed with his commitment to truth and service that Jeanette invited him to join the group. For my part, I could not wait to read his hand, which clearly reinforced the story he had told us. His deep *heart* line went *straight* across his hand, displaying his tendency to keep his feelings close to his own heart rather than trusting others with them. In fact, all of his lines were *deep* and unblemished, except for a big cut below his *pinky* finger, where his *marriage* line would have been. "You were on the phone when you cut yourself," I offered. "I was," he agreed. "In fact, I was talking to my ex-wife." No surprise there.

A relatively deep *fate* line started midway on his hand, indicating that here was a person who was indeed making a considerable discovery at this stage of his life. The fate line crossed his *head* line, and traveled straight up to his *Saturn* (or *middle*) finger. I explained the meaning of the lines to Teddy, who responded, as many people do, by saying that he had never even noticed his hands before and had no idea the markings and lines meant anything at all.

Teddy expressed a desire to know more about how he could stay on the path that God wanted for him. Could I find that information in his hand? "You're on the right path," I replied, pointing out his fate line. Intuitively, I knew that Teddy would establish his camp before this book was published and that all of his lines will continue to deepen as he gives back to life in selfless ways. Though he did not ask, I promised to give a workshop with the kids on self-esteem, something we can easily cultivate by locating the strengths we all possess, which are revealed to us by the markings of our hands.

There is immeasurable return when we give of ourselves to others; though we may not always be aware of it. The following story is the one I tell in response to the question most frequently asked of me: "What is the best reading you ever gave?" To my mind, there is no question that it is the "Egg Salad" story.

Janice was an unemployed, unhappy woman in her early forties who came to me with some urgent questions. A first glance at Janice showed a disheveled person whose hair was uncombed and her clothes askew. She looked as if she had rushed out at the last minute and had been unable or unwilling to prepare herself. As she sat down, I could not help but notice the bits of dried food covering her blouse and the unfortunate decay visible on her front teeth.

I reached for her hand and immediately noticed a few *breaks* in her *life* line and many *chains* on every major line of her hand. These markings indicated that Janice had suffered great duress in several areas of her life. Her life line was *long, clear,* and *well-defined,* however, and this revealed that she would live a long life if she were able to grapple with life's obstacles successfully. As always, I took a few moments to breathe and meditate, requesting that Janice join me before we continued. The *coarse* skin of her hand would make it harder, I knew, for her to take this leap with me, since she was so obviously not influenced by her physical surroundings.

"Janice," I began, "I know that you've come to see me today with many questions in mind. You want to know why there's no love in your life, and if there will ever be someone for you. You want to know why you can't keep friends and why you suffer constant illness in your life." "No!" she said abruptly. "Those are not the questions I wrote down last night!" Given her excited state, I asked Janice to tell me her specific questions—something I rarely do. Most often, those questions are answered in the course of a reading, and my clients are always surprised when they realize that their questions, which had not been spoken aloud, are answered. In this case, however, Janice went on, "When will I get married? What's wrong with my sister—why won't she talk to me? When will I get a job? Will the Lyme disease go away?"

Like many people, Janice was unable to really *see* herself or, quite obviously, *hear* the meaning behind her own words. I took another deep breath and, guided by the powers that be, continued, "Janice, before you look outside of yourself for answers, you need to look *at* yourself. Begin with that egg salad stain on your shirt and your unkempt hair. It's obvious that you need to see a dentist. I am wondering why you have come to see me, since you seem only to want to fight with me. If you listen closely, the questions I thought you wanted answers to are in fact the ones you just asked. And the truth is, *you*, not I, possess the answers you seek."

We spoke for a while about some of the tenets of this book—beginning with truth, desire, prayer, and surrender, and then gratitude—discovering that these simple ideas were sorely lacking in Janice's daily life. She had almost completely squandered a trust fund, which had led to terrible anxiety about supporting herself, and in her own words, her life "was falling apart."

Literally, Janice needed to "clean up her act." I suggested that she take responsibility for her fate by taking care of herself and using some of the ample energy at her disposal, which was presently being wasted on anxiety and negative thinking, by helping those less fortunate. She looked at me wide-eyed, with utter disbelief that I would say such a thing, and I told her that she needed to stop complaining about her life and instead change it. Only then would she become more attractive to herself and to others, and only then would romance and a suitable career enter her life.

I asked her to look at the chains on her palms and told her that they would disappear and change as she changed her life. If she followed my suggestions, I promised, not only would her health improve, but so would her spirit. Lastly, I knew that if she were to give of herself, without expectation of reward, she would reap enormous benefits.

I prayed for Janice after she left, knowing that if she had heard even *half* of what I had said to her, her life would change for the better. Several months later, when we bumped into each other in a neighboring town, *I* did a double take. Janice's appearance was now professional and polished; her teeth were bright; she had been working with teenagers at the local community center, which was also where she met the man she was now dating.

We hugged, thanking each other profusely. Janice thanked me for telling her certain truths she had been unable to see and hear, and I thanked her for so much more: for believing in the life of the spirit and, through service, offering it back to the community.

Sometimes, however, the concept of service and what it actually consists of is not quite so straightforward. In the heat of summer, the legal courts of East Hampton are full of small claims cases. The many conflicts over property boundaries have even included the likes of Martha Stewart, who was recently embroiled in battle over some shrubbery that divided her property from her neighbor's. Family squabbles, DUIs, traffic tickets—our little town court fills up with these matters and so requires a service from the community in the form of jury duty.

As fate had it, I was called for jury duty one summer not long ago. I thought to myself that it would be an interesting, if suspense free, experience. I did not doubt for a moment that I would "just know" the outcome of the trial before the particulars were even presented to me. But I dutifully showed up when I was called on and intended to explain my intuitive skills at the first opportunity.

There were about seventy people in the courthouse that morning. It was explained to us that if our names were called, we were to go to another room where a particular case would be explained to us by the attorneys and we might be chosen to serve on that jury. After a few minutes, I was called into another room and promptly questioned about whether I thought there was anything that might prevent me from serving as an impartial juror. In this case, the police had been sent to the scene of a domestic argument after a neighbor had telephoned and complained about the disturbance.

According to the neighbor, a couple down the road had spent the day yelling and screaming; the woman was crying and it sounded as though the man was becoming violent.

The police arrived and tried to arrest the man. By this time, he had physically abused his girlfriend. According to the defense attorney, the police had tried to arrest the man, who resisted them and broke his leg in the struggle. According to the prosecuting attorney, however, the scenario was that while the police were reading the defendant his rights, the intoxicated man fell backward over a chair and broke his leg.

After hearing the case presentation, the attorneys asked each of us if we felt there was anything about this case that would prevent us from judging it fairly, once it went to trial. I, along with all the others, had no conflicting issue with the case as described. Jury selection then began. When I was called to the stand, the defense attorney proceeded to question me. "Ms. McCue, can you tell us about yourself please? Are you presently married?" "Yes," I replied. "Is this your first marriage?" I said it was. "Do you have any children? Who are the people currently living in your home?" "Yes," I replied once more, "my husband and two sons live with me." "Are you employed?" He continued. "Yes, self-employed." "And what kind of work do you do?" I replied that I was a consultant.

"What do you consult about?" He asked. "I would call myself an intuitive consultant." "What's that?" He pressed. I asked him if he knew who Faith Popcorn was, which caused some people in the room to laugh. Faith Popcorn is a local future trends consultant who is quite well known. "To put it simply," I continued, "you could call me a psychic." More people began to laugh, and I began to get red in the face. "Really? Well, in that case, I guess you can tell me how this case is going to turn out."

It was obvious that the defense attorney was now enjoying himself—at my expense. "Well, sir," I replied, "like yourself,

I do not get involved in matters like this unless I am getting paid for it." Now, everyone in the entire room was laughing. It was the lawyer's turn to get red in the face. "I've never met a psychic before," he said. Then he asked me if I could tell the difference between the facts that were presented to me and my so-called psychic ability. He asked the question in a slow, condescending way, as if I were mentally slow or developmentally disabled. I responded by telling the attorney that my psychic ability was a *gift*, not a mental illness! Of course I could understand the facts as they were presented to me. Those in the courtroom laughed once more, and the attorneys and judge held a short conference.

"You are excused, Ms. McCue," the defense attorney stated. As I rose to leave my seat, I passed the defendant, his broken leg propped up on a chair in front of him. With a glance at his hand and face, I knew in an instant: "By the way, he's guilty!" I blurted out. Though the defense attorney had condescendingly asked me earlier if I would be able to tell him how the case was going to turn out, I suppose my parting words were exactly what he feared, because shortly afterward the entire prospective jury pool followed me out of the room. The judge had decided to begin again and call an entirely different jury pool together.

Though this story may not be a clear-cut example of providing service, I feel that that is in fact what occurred. The most important service I provided was to tell the truth as I saw it in relation to the case. Perhaps next time around, the defense attorney will treat a person with a career or life path so apparently different from his own with less condescension. (By the way, an impartial jury did indeed find this man guilty.)

One winter when I was twelve years old, snowdrifts that were nearly six feet high blanketed Syracuse after one of its classic blizzards. We could barely open the door to the house, the drifts were so deep. I began shoveling our driveway with one of my brothers, and then we shoveled the driveways of our older neighbors, who were obviously stranded at home. We soon found out that Mr. Truttlelot, who was nearing eighty, needed dog food for Max, his German shepherd. The Williams family down the road had a house full of eleven children who needed milk. And the O'Neills had newborn twins in need of diapers. My brother and I soon made a game of seeing how many people we could help. The day was bright and the snow sparkled, and as we cleared the way to our neighbors' houses, we were filled with hope and wonder. Though we were offered tips, we did not take them, simply helping others made us feel incredibly good.

As I grew up, I witnessed how people behaved during crises. I learned how natural it is for us to help our fellow man. When I was living in New York City in the late 1970s, there was a blackout in the middle of a horrendous heat wave. The streets went black, and the air conditioners fell silent. In this stunning stillness, my neighbors and I began helping each other in the dark. Until then, we had not even acknowledged one another. As an ambulance siren screamed amid the chaotic traffic on York Avenue, I began directing traffic so that the ambulance could get through. I've never forgotten that moment or the incredible feeling of love we experience when our hearts open up and we give service to each other.

This spirit of giving is a gift to ourselves as well as to others. We are able to keep our gifts only when we give them away—something I learned very clearly in what I earlier called the "Egg Salad" story.

I was lucky enough to be with a group of people who met Mother Teresa when she made a trip to New York City in the mid 1980s. She was visiting a center that cared for infants and young children who had been born with AIDS. It was an emotional moment for everyone as we watched her care for these ailing young children. I was even more emotional because I had just become a mother for the first time. Breathless, I stood and watched as this frail elderly woman illuminated a room full of hopelessness with the enormous love she felt for these children that nobody wanted. After she greeted and held each of the children, she greeted the adults. She shook our hands and gave us each a small card that she called her business card, which read:

> *The fruit of silence is Prayer,*
> *The fruit of prayer is Faith,*
> *The fruit of faith is Love,*
> *The fruit of love is Service,*
> *The fruit of service is Peace.*

Mother Teresa had honored the divinity in each and every one of those innocent children just as she did for the throngs of people she met the world over. Her exemplary life of service is proof of how an open heart destroys narrow-mindedness and creates love. When we lift a hand to serve others, to help or console another human being, we are lifting the hand of God himself, for God is the embodiment of compassion.

But compassion does not always come easily to us. When we are overwhelmed by our own needs, we easily lose sight of the needs of others. I have several regular callers on my television show, many of whom are senior citizens. One such caller, Rose, who is eighty-seven, phones frequently. Just as we were about to go to a break one day, Rose called. "How are you, Rose?" I asked. "Not too well," she answered, her voice weak. Rose wanted to make an appointment with me, but I assured her that she did not need to—I would answer any questions she had, free of charge. Rose hesitated, then told me she was afraid to go to see any of her doctors because "they always want to operate on me." But, she admitted, she felt a numbness in her feet and was now having trouble walking.

"Would it be better if someone went with you?" I asked, thinking that a neighbor would surely accompany her. "Would you go, Donna, really? I trust you." For a moment, I was dumbfounded; an instant later, I agreed to go. She made an appointment for the following week, and during that time I noticed how much I dreaded that appointment: *What have I gotten myself into? I've got the kids to handle and deadlines to meet. Where are my boundaries? I can't be taking everybody who calls my show to the doctor.*

As I complained to myself again and again that week, another voice piped up behind this anxious, worried one: *Of course I will take her; I want to help her.* Still conflicted on the day of the appointment, I drove to Rose's retirement mobile-home park, and as soon as I saw the tidy little trailer and the sweet flowers she had planted outside her door, my heart melted. Rose, a tiny woman of barely ninety pounds, opened the door with a huge smile. As we waited later for the test results after Rose had seen the doctor, Rose turned pale with fear. I promised I wouldn't leave her. The doctor soon told us that if Rose had waited any longer before seeking treatment, it would have been necessary to remove her gangrenous leg.

That was the day Rose became my teacher. The lesson I learned is that we cannot really know how we can make a difference in someone's life, but each day, the opportunity and choice to serve others is available to us.

WEEKLY EXERCISE

Giving Back

There are parts of this country that often experience flash floods, tornadoes, hurricanes, or earthquakes. Many parts of the world are at war, and as I write this, we hear gloomy, dire news of Kosovo, Yugoslavia. When we are faced with crises of enormous magnitude, we often feel that there is nothing we can do about it. But we can. And that action begins with changing how we *see* the world. If we believe that we can make a difference, we have taken the first step needed to positively change and influence the world around us.

The truth is, if we practice giving, we strengthen the source of our spirit and soul. Imagine, then, that you are a philanthropist. What would you do all day if you had the capacity to truly give on a large scale? Who would you support, and why? Begin a journal and write a list or a story about it now.

Next, write how you might give to others with your special talents. (You will learn how to uncover them in the chapter called "Willfulness: The Thumb.") Write down those traits that are particularly *you*. Now consider your *life* line. What is it telling you about yourself? Make note of those particular characteristics that have just been introduced or clarified for you during the reading of this chapter.

Putting pen aside, realize that the act of giving of yourself extends beyond the page. It is now time to take action. By doing so, I can guarantee that you will begin to know your deepest, most intuitive self. Remember, the simpler the action, the better. You may wish to give an hour a week to a needy cause such as a local charity or senior citizens' center. Or, try just listening to a person who wants to talk even if you think it may bore you. In ten minutes, you may help dramatically change someone's life through this simple gesture of kindness. Make an effort to hold a baby that has nobody, like those HIV-positive infants Mother Teresa showered love upon. In our own small ways, every day we can emulate this great woman's selflessness. We can do this by making a commitment to give service in some capacity to a church, a school, a synagogue, or a hospital.

If you can give by tithing to a religious organization or charity, please do. Tithing is a simple concept that works as follows: give ten percent of your salary to the charity or church of your choice. For me, the act of tithing has an almost mythical power, for I remember this idea from show business days, when I gave ten or twenty percent of my earnings to my agent. Spiritual law states that "As you give, so shall you receive." I have always tried to give a portion of my earnings to various charities, and I've eventually come to think of *God* as my agent! And I can attest to the enormous return I get on this investment. I feel it each time someone takes my hand and says, *"Thank you,"* for in that gesture, I am aware that my life line is literally connected with the other person's, which means that in that moment I am that much more connected to life itself.

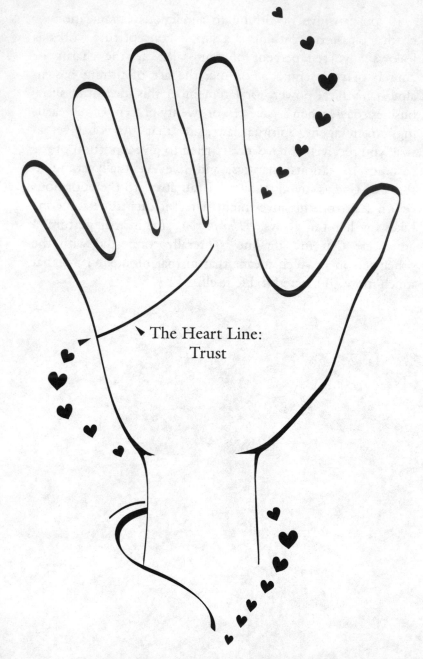

The Heart Line:
Trust

Our Emotions Find Expression on the Heart Line.

FIVE

Trust: The Heart Line

ocated just beneath your fingers and extending across the width of your hand between the *pinky* and *third* (or *index*) finger, the *heart* line reflects your ability to express emotions with immediacy and certainty, often because part of you is aware of being guided by a higher power. Being able to articulate our feelings clearly and with respect and integrity indicates a very healthy relationship to the present moment and reality. But to be this present, we must have a deep and abiding commitment to the truth, and this takes a tremendous amount of faith, a tremendous amount of trust. We can gauge our level of trust by reading our heart line.

Suzanne, a soft-spoken classics professor, had tried repeatedly to become pregnant. This was an unusually frightening proposition for her since Downs syndrome ran in her family. For several years, Suzanne had devoted much time and energy to developing her spiritual life, and when she turned

67

forty-two, she finally conceived a child. However, her doctor vehemently warned her against having the baby.

During our session, Suzanne was on edge, gripped by doubt. "I know what I want. I just don't know if what I want will turn out okay." I suggested that she trust the unfolding process of life, taking note of the fact that I thought it was no accident that she had finally become pregnant after years of trying. Her *heart* line was clear of obstacles at this point in her life, and it stopped on the *Mount of Saturn* (under her middle finger), indicating that she was truly blessed. Not only was she destined to be satisfied in all areas of her life, she was capable of calling upon an inner serenity on which she could rely (though there was evidence of scattered energy and a love of adventure in her past, indicated by the presence of *tassels* and *wavy* lines). Her hands were *square,* indicating her persistent nature, and quite *soft,* revealing a healthy emotional sensitivity.

My only advice for Suzanne was to find another doctor so that she might feel more confident about proceeding with the pregnancy. And to follow her heart's desire. Suzanne did switch doctors, and nine months later, she delivered a beautiful, healthy baby girl.

All Suzanne had to do was *trust* the process, to trust that nature would take care of her baby and trust her own instinct that giving birth to this child was the appropriate course of action to take.

My own experience has shown me that our actions are just as important as, and at moments even more important than, our beliefs. After leaving home and finishing high school in upstate New York, I moved to New York City to become an actress. I landed my first acting job as an extra in *Midnight Cowboy,* where I played a party girl befriended by Andy Warhol's Viva, who played herself. One night, I attended a cast party on the Upper West Side. This was long before any gentrification had occurred, and the neighborhood was then considered quite dangerous, especially after nightfall.

I was fashionably dressed for the event: platform python boots and a denim miniskirt. When I left the party at about three A.M., I accidentally began walking west rather than east. There was not a cab in sight, nor a soul on the dimly lit streets. The only sound I heard was my own breathing until I heard footsteps coming quickly toward me from behind. My heart pounded as I turned to see who was behind me—a tall man with a nylon stocking on his head that held his pompadour in place, a black leather jacket, and boots with chains hanging from them.

It might have been a scene right out of *Midnight Cowboy*. At first I wanted to run, but instead the voice inside me told me not to. I turned around and let the stranger catch up to me. "I'm scared," I said, gripping my handbag with all my might. "I know I'm lost. This looks like a bad neighborhood, and you look like a gentleman. Would you please help me find a cab?" The words came out without a breath. It was my own voice, but in that moment something else other than my conscious mind was guiding me.

I will never forget the surprised look on the man's face. "You're right," he said. "This is a bad neighborhood. Let's get you a cab."

Between my python boots and the stocking on this character's head, taxis began passing us by. Finally, after I loosened the death grip on my bag and stuck out my thumb as a hitchhiker would, a taxi stopped and my escort and I said goodbye to each other.

At the time, I was amazed. Not only by how the situation turned out, but by the insistence of the voice inside me, which had directed my actions. As life goes on, I have learned to pay more attention to this voice, and I fully trust that it will always guide me to safety. A glance at my *heart* line today reveals a deep, clear expanse, which suggests the passion for life I feel and the resilience I now have. My heart line is now free of the early obstacles, indicated by the unbroken *chains* and *islands,* I faced in my youth.

What is most profound about trust is really very simple. We can begin to embrace it by trusting what our own hands tell us.

Dots, while never a positive sign, appear on the *heart* line to indicate periods of ill health. *Breaks* in the heart line can mean several things: illness, a change of events, emotional trauma. Similarly, *islands* suggest a break in a partnership or a change, usually in a romantic relationship.

Sometimes, the heart line may break off and connect with the *head* line. This is called the *Simian* line, as it is a characteristic of other primates, but it represents a single great passion—love, hobby, career—held by its bearer. To many with this line, the approach to love is more physical than emotional.

Descending branches reveal disappointment in love. *Ascending branches* indicate good fortune and, depending on their stopping place on the palm, also point to luck in love, fulfilling partnerships, and personal achievement. Similarly, *tassels* at the end of your heart line denote ambition and likely success; you are usually filled with hidden drive and persistence. However, you may also tend to crave, but mistrust, love.

An ascending branch that ends in a *triple* tassel reveals a very artistic nature. Artists and writers—and more rarely, doctors—possess this line. In love and relationships, these individuals are usually loyal, despite being constantly desired by others.

In regard to the *length* and *depth* of the heart line, an *aver-*

age line extends to the *Jupiter* (or *index*) finger. A *typical* line ends under the index finger and has no branches, indicating a temperament prone to consistency when giving affection and also balance in relation to love.

As discussed earlier, those who possess a *short* heart line, free from obstacles, are promised particular happiness; similarly, a line that extends and rises toward the index finger points to increased power and enjoyment of life. A *pale, wide* heart line indicates a tendency toward sentimentality, but trust may come easily to those of you with this type of heart line.

The healthiest lines are *straight* and *clear* of obstacles, revealing a clarity of emotions and a passionate nature. The *deeper* and more *defined* the heart line, the stronger the heart, both emotionally and physically.

Curious about palmistry and intuition, Daphne, a successful newspaper reporter in her mid forties, decided to write an article about me. I suggested that we do a reading so that she might write from her own experience. When she sat down in my office, tense and abrupt, her hand revealed much more about Daphne's behavior than she understood.

As soon as I touched her *small, chubby* hand, I knew that she had big plans for her life, and that she loved to eat well. Daphne's *heart* line, populated with several *descending branches,* went completely across her hand, revealing a certain single-mindedness—useful in business, but less useful in love. The *straightness* of the line revealed her cautiousness toward romance, and the *descending* branches indicated that she had experienced many disappointments in love. Yet it was her *life* line, connected by *chains* to her *head* line, that gave me the most crucial information, which was that Daphne had remained in a negative relationship for far too long. Her eyes widened when I told her this, and she began to reveal information about her boyfriend that she usually kept hidden from the rest of the world.

Daphne had been living with a man who didn't work and didn't even drive a car. She had supported him for ten years. It was clear that Daphne did not trust herself when it came to love and that she felt she had to settle for second (or third) best. In her own words, "A bad choice is better than nothing."

After the reading, Daphne wanted to talk about Victor, about her fear that if she were to let him go, she might pick another man just like him. Unfortunately, this kind of insecurity is typical of many women who struggle to remain partnered, no matter how damaging the relationship they are in. Daphne admitted that she did not feel worthy of a healthy relationship, nor did she trust herself enough to feel that she could go it alone.

When I talked to Daphne about learning to love herself, it was as if I were speaking in a foreign language, and it was clear to me that she had been ignoring her own truth for many years. Daphne's desires seemed long forgotten, and when I mentioned God, she merely shook her head. I was not surprised that Daphne had no concept of spiritual surrender and what rewards it might bring, but she clearly wanted to talk about it all. In fact, our session ran an extra hour, and when Daphne left, the defensive demeanor with which she had entered my office was completely gone. In its place was a heart and mind that had opened wide enough to hold the many questions Daphne had finally begun to ask herself.

Trust, a basic human need, is essential to our existence if we are to experience fully realized lives. Without a doubt, being able to trust ourselves and others forms the very basis of our sense of security in this world. But because many of us have had our sense of security challenged in many ways, our relationship to trust often needs work and healing.

Art, now a talented interior decorator in his late twenties, is both ambitious and fearful. Rather than striking out on his own, Art has always aligned himself with older, more successful business partners, some of whom became his lovers. Art chose to consult with me after his father died and left him a substantial amount of money.

Like Daphne's, Art's *small* hands told me that he had big plans for his life. Also similar to Daphne's, Art's straight *heart* line signaled his cautiousness toward romance. *Ascending branches* near his *Jupiter Mount* indicated good fortune and a promising relationship to finances. His *life* and *head* lines, however, connected by deep, unbroken lines, revealed his fearfulness in relation to how he was perceived by others. This connection also revealed Art to be loyal, but his insecurity could cause him to be loyal to those who did not merit Art's trust.

I felt it was no accident that his father had left Art money at this time in his life, for Art had already, though tentatively, begun to trust the unfolding of his life. Though it would certainly be a risk for Art to establish his own business, taking that action would free him of the very real constraints he had created for himself by getting involved romantically with his business partner, an older man who tightly held the purse strings of their business.

Art possessed the clarity to face certain truths about himself, and he could now, for the first time, acknowledge his desire to be independent. Our reading revealed that Art had been praying for the courage to surrender to the truth of his life so that he could take the next step and leave his business partnership. But for some reason, he just could not trust himself enough to do so. What, I wondered, was in his way? After the reading, Art told me that he had long hidden his homosexuality from his father, because he was afraid that his father would not only judge him, but disown him. During his father's illness, however, Art had revealed the truth, and his father responded by telling Art that he loved him and was proud of him regardless of his sexual orientation.

It became painfully clear to me that it was Art who did not

love himself unconditionally. Being different from others often inhibits us from trusting that we—and they—will be okay with who we are. As infants, we come into the world wanting to give and receive love. Many of us forget this basic aspect of our being, as we veer off course when life presents us with very real challenges. While it was clear to me that Art had the ability to do wonderful things with his life, it was certainly up to him, as it was up to Daphne, to take the course of his life into his own hands.

Human beings, endlessly varied on the outside, are greatly alike beneath the surface. What was similar about Daphne and Art, aside from the straight *heart* line each client possessed, was that each had hidden a very essential part of themselves. As a result, both of them had to face a major challenge, learning that trust is an active, not a passive, process.

When I look at my own hand, I may become discouraged, even paralyzed, by its markings—various *islands, chains, descending forks,* and *branches*—if I do not remind myself that my challenges and limitations are nothing more than opportunities for growth and self-awareness. If it is impossible for me to see them this way, the very least I can do is acknowledge that God never gives me more than I can handle—spiritually, physically, or emotionally.

Despite what we may believe when challenging circumstances pervade our lives, God does not exist merely to baffle or betray us. But it is often during these challenging times that we turn away from God and begin to hide certain aspects of ourselves, unwittingly redirecting our journey onto a dark and lonely path. In so doing, we not only prevent the light of self-knowledge from leading us forward, but we fail to acknowledge and honor God's presence in our lives.

A work that illustrates this concept perfectly is the well-known poem "Footprints," in which a man dreams that he is walking down a beach with God. Scenes from his life flash before him. In each scene, he notices two sets of footprints in the sand, one set belonging to him and the other to God, except on those occasions when he was most sad or upset, when only one set of footprints appeared. Feeling betrayed, he questioned God about what he perceived as his abandonment. God answered that he had never left the man, for it was in those darkest moments that he had carried the man.

While the concept of trust is enormously complex, its manifestation can be surprisingly simple. I remember how my first son, Danny, loved to jump from the staircase into the arms of his father, who would wait expectantly below. Danny would jump again and again, secure in the knowledge that his father would catch him. That was trust at its most visible. But many of us, at some time in life, have had personal, professional, or romantic experiences that have affected our ability to trust with such surety and unconscious abandon. The mere idea of trusting someone or something can be oppressive. It's as if an invisible and fierce force challenges us and tries to influence us against seeing the universe as a safe and trustworthy environment. To really live in trust, we must cultivate awareness. Truth, desire, prayer, and surrender, all vital road signs, will lead us to deeper, more meaningful living.

Think of trust as a home to the heart; it is where we house our faith in God, in others, and of course, in ourselves. Like so many of our emotions, though, trust may be buried deep within the most closed chambers of our heart. This is the crucial information that is revealed by the heart line, for it plumbs the true depths of our emotional lives. But emotions rarely exist in a vacuum and are often tangled up with many other feelings. For this reason it takes a great deal of self-love, patience, and the willingness to surrender to the truth to untangle them so they may rise to the surface and be set free.

And free us they do, for eternity makes its presence known through trust.

Learning to Trust

As a result of all of our experiences, we arrive at a place of assumption—the assumption that others will treat us as we have been treated, sometimes positively, but more often, negatively. Our challenge, then, comes in admitting the possibility that God will treat us as well as we treat ourselves.

Building our self-esteem is the key to trusting God and our true, psychic, selves. As my own experience has shown me, trust itself is the cornerstone of intuition. How, then, might we approach this state of being? First and foremost, we must do away with self-criticism; rather than telling ourselves what we cannot do, we must begin to tell ourselves what we can do. This week, each time you become aware of a negative thought, take note of it by jotting it down in your journal. Then, both on paper and in your mind, replace it with a positive thought. For example, if your negative thought is, *I drive carelessly,* replace it with something like, *I appreciate my freedom and drive with care*. In effect, you will be *changing* your mind.

Most likely, you will discover by the end of the week that your negative thoughts are most often directed at yourself. The fact is, most self-criticism stems from fear, anger, or insecurity, and only by replacing these emotions with love can we pave the way for trust and the establishment of deep and meaningful connections with others. Learning to love ourselves may sound simple, but most of us have learned to direct our best affections toward others, becoming preoccupied then with how others perceive us. How then, do we begin to love ourselves?

Simple as it may seem, start by thinking of yourself as a guest in your own house this week: fix the meals for yourself that you would serve a guest; make your bedroom and living room as comfortable as you would for others. Next, take yourself out for a meal, a walk, or a new pair of shoes—whatever will provide you with the same sense of satisfaction you'd expect your dearest friend to feel, were you treating that person. Do something nice for yourself *every* day, and pay attention to the negative thoughts that accompany these experiences. Rather than turning away from the experience to avoid these negative feelings, write down the thoughts that accompany it, reminding yourself that in so doing, you are beginning to release yourself from your own obstacles.

As you go through these experiences, pay attention to your hands and, in particular, your *heart* line. Make note of its specific characteristics, such as *chains, branches,* or *forks.* Realize that, depending on where these markings are located on your *heart* line, those that are indicated in the future may indeed change as you do.

Next, work to *change* your behavior. Most of us live within the confines of our own uncertainties. We may not smile at a stranger because we do not trust that the stranger will smile back. This week, go ahead and smile at that stranger, knowing that it really does not matter whether the stranger smiles back: God is with you, guiding you. Disguised in so many ways, opportunities often slip through our fingers because we are too involved with focusing on the results of our actions, rather than on the actions themselves. In actuality, every thought is an opportunity, and so the time has come to *change* our thoughts. As the week begins, choose one thought as the positive theme—the mantra, if you will—for this part of your journey. The thought may be as simple as, *I trust without hesitation with my whole heart* or *God is with me.* Each time you doubt yourself—your actions, thoughts, circumstances, simply repeat this thought. By the end of the week, you may be surprised that you actually believe the idea behind the thought, and you will be that much closer to accepting what *is,* rather than what might be.

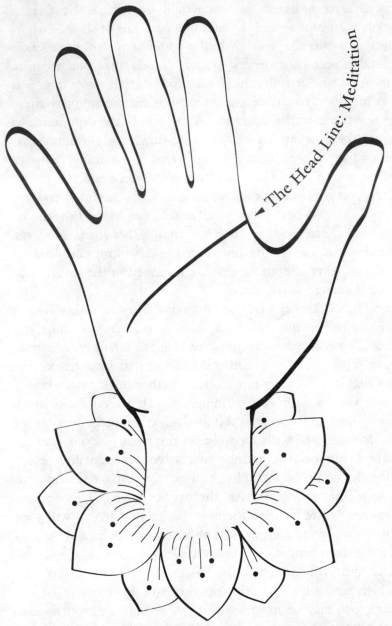

The Head Line: Meditation

Find Concentration and Focus
and the Ability to Meditate Through Your Head Line.

Meditation: The Head Line

The *head* line, found in the center of the hand, starts either at the *Mount of Jupiter* or near or connected to the *life* line and ends close to the *ring* finger or the opposite side of the hand. The head line may either *slope downward*, indicating a good imagination and likely delight in life, or it may cut *straight* across the hand, revealing a determined character that prefers to take calculated risks. If you possess a straight head line, yours is a life with a solid foundation, in which you are able to recognize value when you come upon it.

The *typical* head line ends beneath the *ring* finger. If it ends beneath the *middle* finger, that indicates single-mindedness and a tendency to stay focused until your goal is met; often, people with head lines that end here become specialists of some kind. If the head line extends *beyond* the ring finger, you may likely possess an interest in many subjects and could likely succeed in multiple careers. Finally, a head line that *crosses* the entire hand indicates an intelligent mind and active personality, and if you possess such a head line, you not only have many interests, you are also able to share your enthusiasm with others.

Whether or not the head line is marked is extremely important, because it clearly indicates degrees of concentration and focus you are capable of. A *single, strong* line indicates superb concentration; a line with *chains* reveals a tendency to vacillate in your thinking and may be a sign of an indecisive nature. A *double* head line (two lines running parallel) may represent poor concentration, and this may manifest as an inability to complete tasks or thoughts and to stay committed when the going gets tough. If you have a double head line, you would benefit from a close reading of this very chapter, because meditation will free your mind from distraction. A double line may even indicate a *double life*: you may have two entirely different careers, for example, and you may tend to keep those lives separate, which will prohibit other people from knowing who you truly are.

Clear *breaks* in or *dots* on the head line always indicate some sort of mental trauma; this may be emotional, but often it is career related. A head line that extends to the *outer* edge of the palm may reveal a certain shyness, and individuals with this type of head line may overly rely on reassurance from others. This same individual may, however, gain widespread fame or notoriety in his life's work.

When the head line is *connected* to the *life* line, its bearer is often dependent on the company of others; here is an individual who is attached to family. If your head line *barely touches* the life line, a cautious nature is revealed. You are the type of person who will likely study all your options before acting.

A head line that begins entirely *separated* from the life line indicates an independent nature, though it doesn't indicate a lack of judgment, and you may be hesitant to jump into situations bearing risk. A line that is *widely separated* from the life line reveals a character full of self-confidence. You tend to feel you can do anything you set your mind to. The wider the separation between these two lines, the more confidence you possess.

From all appearances, Jacqueline has a charmed existence. She finished high school at the age of sixteen, graduated from Stanford University with honors, and rose to the top of her class at New York University Law School. Beautiful and accomplished at thirty-three, she is a partner at a Wall Street firm, happily married, and has even found the time to give birth to two young sons.

When people consult with me, they most often wish to learn more about one of three areas of their life: love, career, or health. Jacqueline was the exception. Before our session, I asked her to prepare for the reading, just as I ask every client to, by writing down three questions she wished to have answered. I then asked her to slip that list beneath her pillow the night before the reading. What usually happens is that I find the answers to those questions in my own dreams that very night.

The night before Jacqueline's reading, I dreamed of Barbie dolls. The dreams themselves held no obvious answers, and so I approached our session with increasing curiosity. Jacqueline walked in with a definite air of authority, and I immediately had the impression that when this woman put her mind to something, she achieved the results she sought. Right away, I noticed her *broad* hands, revealing her broad attitude toward life. Here was a person always interested in new concepts and trends. Her *head* line, deeply etched and extending across her whole hand, revealed a strong personality; it was widely separated from her *life* line, indicating independence and confidence, and it ended with a *triple prong*. Jacqueline was fully capable of juggling three careers or maintaining focus on three different areas in her life, such as career, family, and a hobby or outside interest.

Her hand made it even more obvious that Jacqueline was a person who made her own decisions in life, choosing to depend on herself rather than on others, and so I asked her why she had come. She told me that she was not unhappy and that, in fact, everything in her life was fine. In her words, Jacqueline was "perplexed." She had taken some time off to explore the spiritual side of life and had made the choice to work with a teacher, studying Raja or "Royal" Yoga. And so far, she found herself dissatisfied with this practice.

Raja Yoga is a discipline that is over three thousand years old. It has eight prescribed steps and is said to lead the aspirant to an ultimate union with the divine and to enlightenment. In the course of instruction, the teacher, or Yogi, uses specific practices, postures, and breathing techniques that lead to specific changes in consciousness. On the surface, this type of study seemed ideal for Jacqueline's legalistic mind—perform *A,* follow with *B,* and the result will be *C.* The problem for Jacqueline was that she felt she wasn't achieving the desired state of centeredness promised by the method and found herself feeling frustrated rather than at peace. Jacqueline had become skeptical once she had begun to doubt herself; perhaps, she said, she "hadn't accumulated enough merit to advance along this path." Then, she began to doubt the system itself, since other forms of meditative practice had provided her with satisfying results. "Why not this one?" she asked.

As I listened, I recalled the Barbie dolls that had filled my dreams the previous night. When Jacqueline finished explaining her situation, I asked her what significance Barbie dolls had to her. "None," she quickly answered, looking at me skeptically. I asked her to take a deep breath and allow herself to let her mind wander on the subject of the dolls. "Well, I guess I had a few when I was a kid," she began, but then she stopped talking.

I have come to realize that there is no one formula that will provide spiritual enlightenment for everyone, and in this case, Jacqueline was *no* exception. Our expectations can often hinder us rather than help us engage deeply in the meditative process, and so I advised her to ease off on her study of Raja Yoga and replace it with play Barbie dolls. I felt strongly that if she would allow herself to reexperience the freedom and spontaneity that playing with dolls had given her when she was young, she might feel more open and at peace. Unfortunately, this was not the kind of answer Jacqueline was looking for, and she ended the session abruptly. Given her level of self-reliance, I was not surprised, nor did I anticipate hearing from her again.

Six months later, Jacqueline called me. It seems that after she left the reading she had taken half of my advice; she stopped the yoga practice but had forgotten about the dolls. Then, her parents sold their house as they were preparing to move away. They asked Jacqueline and her siblings to either take or dispose of their old belongings. Jacqueline had found her old Barbie dolls in the attic. Remembering our session, she took them home. Feeling foolish at first, she tried to play with the dolls. Nothing happened. After a few moments, however, memories of her childhood began to flood back to her. They were memories of people, places, and events. Soon, these memories drifted into a larger sense of lightness, and she began to feel the sweetness and innocence of childhood, and her playful imagination began to surface. It was then that she began to play with the dolls.

That was the moment, as Jacqueline said, "I finally got it." She had approached her previous study of meditation with all the joy and spontaneity of someone studying the periodic table of elements. Rather than trusting and surrendering to the process of meditation, her ego had maintained control of the experience, so it was impossible for her to experience the "letting go" she desired.

In the end, Jacqueline did not return to study Raja Yoga; rather, she returned to the religion of her youth and found an open and fulfilling path to meditation there.

Over the past thirty years, Western culture has increasingly embraced Eastern ideas and practices of meditation. I must confess that I am old enough to remember when Mia Farrow jumped into John Lennon's psychedelic Rolls-Royce and joined the Beatles on their pilgrimage to India to study Transcendental Meditation with Maharishi Mahesh Yogi. Since that time, it seems there has been no shortage of meditation masters to offer us supposedly newer and better meditation secrets.

While many people are certainly interested in meditation, however, few have a clear understanding of what meditation actually is. Most of us have heard about chakras, mantras, and tantras, for example, but could not explain what they are. At its simplest, meditation is a process of continued awareness that leads us closer to our *source*. There are many names people give to this source—God, soul, spirit, self—but these names don't matter. What counts is our awareness of a spiritual power in our lives. When we come to engage with this power, we will be able to move beyond the five senses, those we rely on to define our relationship to the physical world, and expand our experience of life immeasurably. By the time we become adults, however, many of us believe in the limitations of space and time, and however unconsciously, we accept that there is nothing more to our experience of the world.

Children prove us wrong. My two young boys, Danny and Alex, have repeatedly shown me that we can enter another realm of being simply by making a choice to do so. Danny, the sportsman in the family, can instantly and magically transport himself to the final game of the NBA Championship at

Madison Square Garden and score the winning basket for the Knicks. Alex, our martial arts expert, can fight Bruce Lee and Chuck Norris in a back alley at the same time, and then walk away unscathed. Is this mere child's play? Yes, it is. Are these imaginary games? Yes, they are. Yet where does the capacity to play and imagine come from? My answer is from our *source*.

As we grow older and our egos develop, most of us gradually lose touch with the spontaneous part of ourselves; the practical responsibilities of adulthood loom much larger than the magical part of ourselves, which, sadly, begins to fade with time. The many choices offered to us by our freewheeling culture have, paradoxically, failed to nurture us in relation to the care and development of our relationship to our source, which, I believe, has given rise to our growing interest in meditation.

For many of us, this new interest is accompanied by frustration, for most of us have little idea *how* to meditate, and frequently we aren't patient or determined enough to figure it out. And the fact that there are dozens, even hundreds, of meditation techniques doesn't make this easier for us. Impatience and self-defeating thinking tend to inhibit or even curtail the meditative process because we strive for perfection of technique rather than an open attitude. The fact is, it is much more important to have the right attitude, rather than the right technique, about meditation. And the most promising attitude is one that comprises trust and surrender.

We must first trust the part of ourselves that exists beyond our egos—that is, our source—and we must surrender to it. By *surrender*, I mean that we must avail ourselves of the meditative state without any preconceived expectations; we must allow it to happen to us. Surprisingly, this is the single most difficult concept of meditation for many people to grasp.

Though he had attended an Ivy League college and studied engineering, Jim, an eldest son, had returned home to Long Island to work the farm his great-grandfather had one hundred fifty years ago. Our initial conversation took place on the phone, where Jim revealed that he was interested in learning what the year ahead would bring. I sensed that it would be a year of great upheaval: I saw a relationship ending, an illness, and an opportunity for great wealth. After I said as much, Jim made an appointment for an in-person consultation.

His hands were *large* and *powerful,* which told me that Jim was a person who appreciated the small details in life. What I noticed next was that both his *heart* and *life* lines had significant breaks in the same area, marking the present time in this life. Those breaks indicated a broken heart. His *head* line *sloped* dramatically *downward,* indicating that he was altogether too sensitive and imaginative for his own good; Jim was probably one of the world's biggest worriers. When I mentioned this to him, Jim admitted that he was unable to sleep at night, worrying over his father's health and imminent death from cancer, worrying over the divorce his wife had requested and the effect this would have on his three college-age kids, and the fact that he would need to sell the farm to be able to support them all. Great guilt consumed Jim when he contemplated selling the family legacy, and it had become impossible for him to come to a decision.

Jim's anxiety was palpable. I held his hand and suggested that we do a simple breathing exercise that would help calm him. I told him he would be able to make the decisions he wanted and needed to when he was able to reach the still place inside of himself that would effortlessly speak his deepest truth, but that he had to be willing to meditate at least five minutes a day to reach it. Jim immediately announced that "I tried that, and it doesn't work for me. I don't have any time for it either."

Many clients I've consulted with share Jim's resistance. And it is plain human nature that most of us want results without making much effort. I have come to think of this as the soul's impatience. In Jim's case, I suggested that he did have the time, since he was not sleeping at night, and like the seeds he planted on his farm, it would take time before he was able to reap the benefits of the practice. He smiled ruefully then, but continued to resist the idea. Instead, he chose to tell me that he hated the family business and wished he could just move back to California where he had surfed during the sixties.

"Then think of the California ocean," I said. "Can you see yourself surfing there?" He nodded. "That's all you need to do to meditate," I said, advising him to visualize the sun shining down while he rode the waves. Jim really smiled then. "If you can see it right now," I said, "I have no doubt that a capacity for light and peace is already *inside* you. And so are the answers you seek. Make the attempt to sit quietly for five minutes each day, breathing slowly and visualizing this scene. I promise you, amazing things will happen." Jim finally promised that he would try.

A few years passed before I heard from Jim again. After his father died, he did sell off most of the land, but he kept the family house and ten acres of property for his own family. Jim bought some land in California and was planning to move back to the place where he had surfed as a boy. He also recently met a sufi dancer with whom he had fallen in love, and they are beginning this new life together. "None of this would have happened if I had not meditated. I was so full of guilt about the farm and before, I never would have been open to a woman like Sari." Now, Jim meditates every day, and more than anything else, feels more connected to the *moment* than ever before in his life.

In the stillness of meditation, our deeper self gives rise to our imagination. If we are listening, our true voice can be heard, for it is in this stillness that the realization of the self takes

place. Many of us, however, are just too impatient or overwhelmed with life's challenges to make the time to find the
gifts only meditation can bring.

I first began to meditate in my early twenties when I was
working odd jobs—waitress, bartender, receptionist—to help
support my acting and performing. Although I was not interested in anything but becoming a successful actress at the
time, someone told me that meditation would help me relax
before an audition, a time when I would experience great
anxiety. After I began to meditate, my mind would quiet
down before an audition and I began to feel safe, rather than
anxious, when I took the stage. Though I left my acting
career behind, I have never stopped meditating.

First and foremost, you need to create a quiet space in
which to meditate. I like to light a candle to serve as a beacon
for clarity. I also like to place flowers in the room. By showing
respect for the spirit as well as the beauty of the moment, performing such rituals may ease you toward a meditative state.
If you can and wish to, surround yourself with music, incense,
or photos of wonderful places. Some people choose a favorite
chair in which to meditate, though you may just as readily
choose the floor, for once you are sitting down, it is important to keep your spine erect. Next, close your eyes, and begin
a transition period of about sixty seconds to simply become
still while you leave the hustle and bustle of your daily existence and approach the timeless dimension of yourself.

Next, become aware of your body and begin to visualize it
as a vessel. Outside, your body is covered with clothes, but
inside, as a vessel, it is hollow. Hollow, but filled with a brilliant golden light that is your true self, your eternal being.
After you have kept this visualization in your mind for two or
three minutes, begin to pay attention to your breath: watch it
coming and going. Try to notice how it feels entering and
leaving your nostrils, and become aware of any sensations you
experience as your breath travels down your throat into your

lungs. Notice the part of your breathing when there is no active breath, the part between inhalation and exhalation, and how your breath feels as it leaves your lungs and makes its way back through your nostrils, finally releasing into the universe.

I want to stress how important it is that you not only visualize the light but also experience its warmth flowing through every cell of your body. If you have trouble doing this, try to remember a brilliant sunny day that you have spent at the beach or some other pleasant place. See the sun high in a cloudless blue sky and feel how you are bathed by its warm, caressing rays. Breathe it in, breathe it out. It is essential that you experience these rays as a living and loving force that floods through your skin and fills your entire being, for that is exactly what they do.

After people have tried this particular meditation, some have told me that they had trouble imagining their body as an empty vessel. I have suggested that they find a picture of themselves, preferably a picture from childhood. The idea is to look at the picture and allow any memories, good or bad, to spring forth. Dwelling on those memories for a few minutes is beneficial, for it allows us to step back mentally and begin to view the person in the picture almost as a *third party*. What happens next is that feelings of tenderness and love for that person in the picture arise and we are able to reexperience the innocence and beauty that each of us possesses. These feelings add a deeper, more loving dimension to the practice of meditation.

When they first approach meditation, it is not uncommon for people to balk at what they think of as just an "imaginary" exercise. While the concept of a light existing within us may seem contrived, I can promise that if you continue the practice of meditation, you will find that the *concept* of light becomes a *reality*. Incredibly, the light you find within will become just as real as anything else—your car, your house, your shoes.

Spiritual traditions from various cultures throughout history tell us that we are, essentially, beings of light. Religious art throughout the ages has depicted saints and other holy beings as being surrounded by light. In ancient Egypt, for example, this light was referred to as a *solar disk,* and in Christianity it is known as a *halo.* In the tantric traditions of the near and far east, the light is referred to as the *thousand-petaled lotus of light,* which sprouts from the head of the completely enlightened person. These halos symbolize the realization of their own nature by the enlightened. Even today, when someone has found their source and makes contact with a higher power, we say that person has *seen the light.*

This light is also the common theme that comes up when people talk about their near-death experiences. Professionals like Dr. Elizabeth Kubler-Ross and Stephen Levine have studied countless near-death experiences of people of all ages, social classes, and religious and cultural backgrounds. One common element from these diverse experiences is the sensation of having been in the presence of an incredible light coupled with the feeling of profound unconditional love.

The ancient *Egyptian Book of the Dead,* written three thousand years ago, speaks of this light, as does the *Bardo Thodol* or *Tibetan Book of the Dead.* They both express the idea that the light is an infinite world of calm, love, energy, and beauty, for this is the light from our very source and, therefore, it is always present within us. Unfortunately, many people only become aware of the light as they die, when their physical senses fall away and their awareness is focused on the very center of their being. Meditation is a way to experience the joy and beauty of this remarkable light while still being wonderfully present in this earthly realm.

Entering into a truly meditative state may seem overwhelming at first. If we possess the faith to pursue the light, however, any initial discomfort will disappear. Bearing this in mind, I would like to relate a wonderful story.

There is a sweet, bright young woman by the name of Samantha, who used to baby-sit for my children when she was a teenager. After she graduated high school, she went away to college in Texas. During the summer of her freshman year, Samantha came to my house to visit the children and tell us about her first year in college. She was excited by how much her mind had opened up since she left the security of her home and high school and ventured into the larger world. We talked about many things, but we arrived again and again at how all of these new ideas she had had also resulted in a crisis of faith for Samantha.

In one course, for example, Samantha had studied some scientific theories relating to the origin and size of the universe. This new information had a profound effect on her. She told me that the planet we call home revolves around one of one hundred billion stars in our local galaxy, and that our galaxy is only one of fifty billion other galaxies in the known universe. This all made her feel very small and insignificant, and it directly contradicted her religious beliefs. Samantha felt she could no longer believe that in a universe this vast, there was a single creator who knew and cared about individual beings like herself. For the first time in her life, she felt profoundly alone.

Of course, I acknowledged the premise that the universe is a vast, seemingly immeasurable, awesome place. By its very definition, however, the universe could not be the universe without containing all the elements and parts that it does, from the largest galaxy to the smallest grain of sand on the smallest planet. I suggested that instead of being scared off by the immensity of the universe, Samantha might begin to look at the universe with an open and innocent eye. William Blake's concept of *innocence,* as expressed in his poem "Auguries of Innocence," is what I had in mind:

> *To see a world in a grain of sand*
> *And a heaven in a wild flower,*

Hold infinity in the palm of your hand
And eternity in an hour.

Because Samantha and I came from similar Christian back-grounds, I shared some of my own experience with her. As a child, I was given the image of our creator as some old man with a beard who sat in the clouds in some faraway place called Heaven. I was told that he made some big laws, called Commandments, and that if we wanted to go to this place called Heaven we had to obey all those laws. Even though he sat up in a throne somewhere in Heaven, he knew everything each human being did and even what each person thought. If we broke any of these laws, I learned, God would know immediately and would punish us by sending us to Hell. Simultaneously, I was also told that he loved us very much. As I got older, I outgrew these ideas. But I did not, at the time, have any idea of how I might replace this contradictory or confusing belief system.

My view changed abruptly one summer when I was in my twenties and had the opportunity to travel to Rome. There, I absorbed and studied the architecture and art (and Italian men!). I particularly wanted to see the Sistine Chapel and Michelangelo's famous painting *The Creation of Adam*. My interest was intensified by my studies as a palmist. I was curious to see if I would be able to identify the lines Michelangelo painted on the figures' hands. *Does Adam have a Simian line? What are God's head and heart lines like? Is his life line impossibly long?* These are the questions I asked myself as I approached the chapel.

When I stepped inside the Sistine Chapel, my awe was so immense I was literally dumbstruck; the paintings on that ceiling possessed a sublime, eternal beauty and passion I have never forgotten. Michelangelo Buonarroti has been called the greatest artist of all time by many art scholars, and I would wholeheartedly agree.

In *The Creation of Adam*, God is depicted as an elderly

man with a long beard, supported by angles of light in a brilliant sky. He is leaning over to touch Adam and thus provide
him with the spark of life. It is a powerful, deeply moving
piece of work. The face of God is quite strongly presented in
a loving, paternal way. The questions I came with fell away in
the face of the painting's power. Seeing that painting forced
me to reformulate my ideas about God, and in the end, I
decided that the act of creation wasn't something that happened merely once in all of time, but that creation is happening endlessly. For every one of us possesses the divine spark
of life. And I realized that by meditating on this concept, I
was actually practicing the act of creation every moment.

As Samantha and I sat on the couch talking about these
many ideas, I shared with her that when my mind gets overwhelmed, I often meditate on Michelangelo's masterpiece. I
suggested that she might be able to give her restless, expand-
ing mind some respite and regeneration by trying to do the
same. The next Easter I received a postcard from the Sistine
Chapel, in which Samantha thanked me again for our talk.
The card stated that she was meditating regularly, which had
enabled her to form an ongoing relationship with God and
the power of God's light. Meditation, she wrote, even seemed
to make her goals and dreams possible—she was in Rome,
wasn't she? Finally, she went on to agree that Michelangelo
was, indeed, "divine," and so were other Italian men!

The truth is, we are all "divine." And we can best get in
touch with this truth about ourselves through meditation.

WEEKLY EXERCISE

Beginning to Meditate

This week, open your journal and write the words, *I am a
master of meditation*. Though you may find yourself smiling as
you read that line, you will, in all seriousness, soon believe it.

To begin to meditate, allow your imagination to take over for a period of time and allow yourself to pretend that you are a spiritual teacher. If it helps, visualize yourself surrounded by angels or, perhaps, light candles, burn incense, or play soft music—whatever helps you get in the mood. Take a few moments to massage your *head* line, feeling its grooves and curves and its promise of serenity.

Because you *are* a spiritual master, you are already aware of being in possession of a great body of knowledge. Drawing upon that knowledge, answer the following questions: *What have I learned about the concepts of surrender and trust? How do I continue to resist them in my daily life? Regardless of where I am in this process, am I willing to accept who I am and enter the meditative realm of imagination?*

After you have responded to these questions, no matter what the answers are, you will have displayed a willingness to surrender logic and reason to a power beyond yourself. The characteristics reflected in your *head* line will support this act, since you have actively cleared the path of resistance and are now ready to meditate.

When you start to meditate, simply breathe for five minutes at a time, slowly working your way up to twenty minutes each day. Whatever the time period, simply allow your body to breathe. Do not try to adjust or regulate the breath, merely notice it. Any noises or sensations that accompany the process are perfectly acceptable. Simply witness what is occurring and embrace the feeling of being filled with a warm, golden light. As you become familiar with your own sensations, the light may, or may not, start to follow the circulation of your breath. What is most important is to simply allow your breath to become your focus, to observe it, but surrender your control over it.

Initially, you may wish to set an alarm to let you know when the time for meditation has ended. Soon, however, you will automatically know when it is time to stop. After my own meditation ends, I like to sit still for another two or three minutes, giving thanks in prayer for the wonderful sense of peace I experience, which has often been missing in other areas of my life. It is this sense of peace that reminds me how much I want to live in harmony with myself, my God, and with the world around me.

Because I see so many *islands, dots, horizontal lines,* and *descending branches* on the palms of my clients, I know our negative attitudes toward ourselves must change so that we can lead richer, more satisfying lives. Do you regularly feel aches and pains in particular areas of your body? When you meditate, take note of where your body holds pain and write down the specifics. As you continue to meditate, begin to breathe directly into the blocked areas, noting how your symptoms change as you do so. Paying attention to your body on this basic level is a simple yet essential step, for illness often manifests out of anxiety and stress, rather than as a result of organic influences. Most often, a combination of negative mental and physical factors result in the idea of *dis-ease,* or disease. Our goal, then, is to become more comfortable with ourselves.

As your body responds to the attention you give it while meditating, begin to expand your relationship with it by introducing sources of pleasure, such as warm baths, long walks, and consistent exercise. Not only will you feel more relaxed, you may even sleep better. As time passes, your body will provide messages for you of comfort or discomfort, and you will learn to trust those messages. If your heart pounds when your lover enters the room, you will experience the feeling with delight; if your stomach aches as you walk into a job interview, you will recognize the feeling as anxiety. No longer blocking the messages of the body, you will come closer to your intuitive self. Ultimately, you will learn to *believe* yourself, which is not only one of life's greatest gifts, but the very cornerstone of intuition.

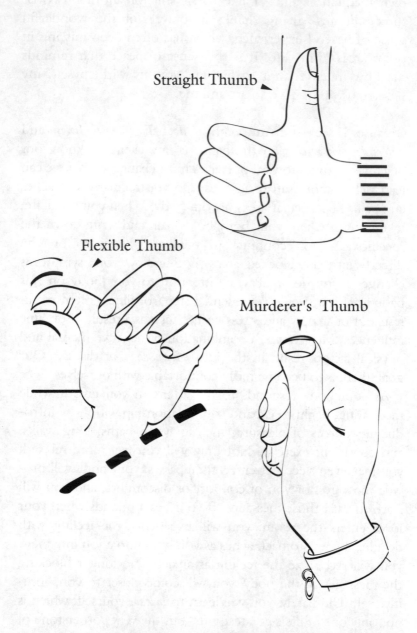

Straight Thumb

Flexible Thumb

Murderer's Thumb

Your Thumb Reveals How Willful You Are.

SEVEN

Willfulness: The Thumb

The adult thumb offers a range of movement and dexterity that is particularly human, symbolizing our capacity to conquer adversity and to succeed in building strength of character by sheer force of will. The thumb is also the part of the hand that reveals our relationship to logic and reason, which sets us apart from other animals. Evolutionary biologists credit much of our species' advancement to our "opposible thumb," because it gave us the ability to manipulate our environment by picking things up with precision. With the thumb, we can impose our will on the world. Willpower and reason can work against us, however, when our egos begin to rule our experience, interfering with our understanding of truth.

When you look at your own thumb, what do you see? Is it straight, bent back, or relaxed? Does it get tense when you are nervous or under stress, or do you grip your thumbs with your other fingers? Those of us who hide or cover our thumbs at these moments are exhibiting a classic protective reaction. In more extreme instances, adults experiencing certain types of severe emotional disturbance and babies hide their thumbs in clenched fists, clearly exhibiting their lack of control over circumstances.

For the majority of us, however, there are several other possibilities in our grasp. And while we cannot change the actual genetic structure of our thumbs or our hands, we can change the way we use our will, or avoid using it, in our lives. When we do accept ourselves, we may find that our thumbs return to their natural state, that is, they become more relaxed or less rigid.

The thumb, like the fingers and the palm itself, gives us clear information about ourselves as individuals, but only if we are listening. A *narrow, pointed* thumb reveals a tendency toward insecurity and difficulty with staying powerful in the face of conflict or a moment of decision making.

Bebe, a client of mine with a *narrow* thumb, wanted to rid herself of a boyfriend who also managed her restaurant and finally offered a severance package to him, which was the only thing that convinced him to leave. But her thumb also stuck out like a *hitchhiker's*, indicating a stubborn streak and strong will. In this particular case, the combination of these elements worked against her. I want to stress that this did not happen because Bebe had a thumb whose innate characteristics led to misfortune, but that it was Bebe herself who refused to accept the truth of her relationship *after* learning about the tendencies she embodied during our session together. She later admitted that her deep desire to be in a relationship had overwhelmed all reason, and that even though she realized mixing business with pleasure was far from wise, her will had led her astray.

The thumb, however, promises other experiences. A *strong* thumb that *angles backward* in hitchhiker fashion exhibits a sense of staying power, altruism, and leadership, yet its bearer may tend to translate thought into action prematurely or impulsively. President Clinton has such a thumb and has proven that leadership ability does not necessarily exclude stubbornness and inflexibility. Just look at what happened following Mr. Clinton's unfortunate denial of his liaison with Monica Lewinsky.

Then there is the thumb that looks entirely *straight* and *strong*; this thumb belongs to a person who is not easily swayed by changing events and circumstances. Acting on their own will and telling the truth is second nature to the bearer of this type of thumb.

A *long* thumb implies a natural ability to accomplish desired goals, but do not be surprised if its owner tends to stay up into the middle of the night, perhaps writing or plotting some kind of creative act; sometimes these people go a bit too far without realizing it. For those of you with this kind of thumb and/or tendency, I suggest that you work on the idea of *surrender*, which I will say more about later.

A thumb with a *clubbed tip* belongs to someone prone to impatience who may use their own will to skirt the truth. If yours is such a thumb, you need to begin to control the scattered energy that leads you to inadvertently rush past your goals. You can do this by slowing down and breathing more fully. Physical exercise will surely help.

Similarly, there is a so-called *murderer's thumb*, usually a *thick, bulbous* thumb, which indicates that its bearer is truly untrustworthy. In my entire career I have seen only two thumbs like this, and each bearer did, indeed, have a "checkered past." One of those people was a criminal, and the other a therapist who, after grappling with her own will, had transformed her life by telling the truth about her misdirected past. Succumbing to sexual promiscuity at a very early age, she began a career as a sex worker, and her experiences led her down some dark, dangerous roads. After seeking professional help that enabled her to face the truth of her shadowy experiences, the world opened up to her, eventually leading to her present path, becoming willing to help battered women put their lives back together.

A *knotty* thumb denotes a strong and imaginative personality. For those of you with this kind of thumb, telling the truth could be a big challenge in your life because your fantasies are often bigger than reality, and so you are apt to deny your own will and the truth altogether. How might this passionate personality begin to approach these concepts? More so for you than anyone else, your first step is to complete the exercises at the end of this chapter, on *using will to find the truth*, and to begin to accept life on its actual terms.

A *flexible, supple* thumb indicates a generous person, one who gives freely of time, money, even sympathy. This is a person who loves to entertain and is very drawn in by drama, as if trying to prove that the concept of will or the truth is less important than the drama itself. Beware of this tendency, which will keep you from staying grounded. Though it may sound too simple, what you revelers need to do is to stay in *the body*; this can be achieved by looking, not in a crystal ball, but in a mirror. You can also become aware of your body by walking in a heavy-footed way, being conscious as your feet reach the ground. Engaging in sports, such as running or soccer, would be helpful, as long as your feet stay on the ground.

Regardless of shape or size, a *stiff* thumb indicates a tendency to budget both time and money and a desire to control the flow of each. The positive element here is self-control, but the negative elements, rigidity to the point of missing opportunities and having to be right at all costs, may severely limit your experience. Chances are, you would benefit from relaxing into what *is*, instead of focusing on what should be, and allowing yourself to dream a few new dreams.

Because of the thumb's unique capabilities, it is the only one of our digits that can function well on its own. It is also one part of our bodies that most of us take for granted, only real-

izing its premier importance when we have the misfortune to
injure it.

Last summer I attended a party where I met a man who
had lost all four fingers of his right hand. While I felt sad for
his loss, I was extremely interested in reading his hand for
that very reason. Mitch was a handsome man in his early thirties with a classic, strong jawline. What made his hand truly
unique was that all of his fingers had been cut at the base,
extending beyond the mounts of each finger. Though Mitch
had been right-handed before he severed his hand in an accident, he now wrote with his left hand.

I first focused on the thumb of his right hand, which was
straight and *strong*, alerting me that Mitch was someone not
easily influenced by events or situations, and that he was comfortable with hearing and telling the truth. Too, Mitch's *heart*
line traveled in a *deep, straight* path across his palm, revealing
a fair nature, capable of loyalty and true friendship. His heart
line was marked only by an *island* in the area that coincided
with adolescence. I sensed that the island, indicating depression, had something to do with the loss of his fingers.

Mitch's *head* line was also *deep*, curving toward the *Mount
of Luna*, which suggested a well-developed intellect and possible artistic ability. His *life* line had a *break* in it, revealing
once more a severe trauma that had taken place, again coin-
ciding with adolescence. "You severed your hand in an accident, didn't you? You were working with power tools when
you were about sixteen years old, but you got into trouble
when you didn't ask anyone how to use them. Your own will
took precedence over wisdom." Mitch's eyes opened wide.
"Did our hostess tell you that?" I shook my head. "You were
depressed after that and thought your life was over." "That's
exactly right," Mitch said. "I wanted to be a baseball player!"
"My feeling is that you're involved with drawing and draft-
ing. Are you an architect?" I asked. He nodded. "And sometimes you feel self-conscious because women are turned off

by your hand." He continued to nod. "That's right. But I always say it could have been even worse . . . it might have been another part of me that was cut off." We both laughed.

I told Mitch that his sense of humor and willingness to overcome the loss of his fingers had given him a bigger gift than he could ever have imagined. He might never have developed his drawing skill at all, for example, and he agreed completely. Mitch explained how he was able to use both hands in his work, and how his thumb had taken over the work of many fingers. As he talked, it became clear that his life had become richer in ways that baseball could not have provided.

Finally, it was obvious to me that Mitch might never have had to develop the willingness to look unflinchingly at the truth had he not been constantly faced with the reactions of others to his unique situation. "You know, when a woman is turned off just because you don't have a couple of fingers, you can see that she's not the one for you anyway." "So thumbs down to her," I added, and we both laughed again.

The thumb is named after Rhea, one of the oldest, most universal goddesses. In the Aegean pre-Greek cultures, she was known as the Great Goddess, or the Great Universal Mother. When Hellenic invaders arrived, they tried to suppress her worship by imposing patriarchal gods, but soon found that they could not and were ultimately unsuccessful. Not surprisingly, then, the thumb, the great indicator of will, was named after her.

Over the years, Rhea became known by several different names, for she had several different functions. She was Aega, the founder of the Aegean civilization; Cictynna, the lawgiver; Britomartis, the virgin, and Rhea Kronia, or Mother Time.

Rhea is also known as the Universal Goddess. To the Celts, she was Rhiannon, or Mother Time, and she is said to have devoured her own children; the ancients of Russia called her Rha, the Red One; the Hindus called her the Great Goddess Kali, the Mother of Time whose red dress symbolizes the blood of her devoured children. In many parts of Asia Minor, she was known as Cybele.

According to classical Greek mythology, Gaea, or the Earth, came out of the darkness at the beginning of time. She was barren and alone. Uranus, or the Sky, became her lover, and Earth became Mother Earth. Her first children were called Titans. Cronus, her youngest and strongest, became Lord of the Universe. He took Rhea for his wife. Cronus had usurped the power of the throne from his father and, after that act, became afraid that one of his own children would do the same to him. Consequently, he swallowed every one of Rhea's newborns. Heartbroken, Rhea finally asked Mother Earth for advice. She was told that as soon as she gave birth again, she should hide the child, wrap a stone in baby clothes, and hand it to her husband. She followed the advice, fooled Cronus, and gave life to Zeus, who survived and was raised by Mother Earth in a cave on the Greek island of Crete.

This wonderful story illustrates the indomitable power of will. It seems fitting, then, that Rhea, the *thumb* (and will), stood in opposition to her husband Cronus, the *middle* finger (or time), her son Jupiter, the *index* finger (or the sky), and her grandson Apollo, the *ring* finger (or light).

As we have seen, our will can work for us and against us. Perhaps more than anything else in my life, I have wanted to be loved. Beginning at a very early age, the wish that other people might convince me of my worth has influenced my ability to see my own truth, that I am lovable. I am reminded of this in my weakest moments in unexpected, even glorious ways. One such instance was when I ran into Sister Mary Angelis, the kindergarten teacher whom I had not seen in over twenty years. I was sitting in a beautiful cathedral in San

Francisco, weeping. A relationship had just ended, and I had gone to the cathedral to pray, feeling so sad and utterly lonely until a shadow appeared behind me—Sister Mary Angelis. The light was streaming down through the stained-glass windows in a way that made it look as if God were trying to reach out to me personally, which I believe he was. He had sent Sister Mary Angelis to comfort me again, just as she had in kindergarten.

At four and a half years old, I was a precocious, talkative child, someone looking for a lot of attention. Because I could write my name, my mother placed me in kindergarten at the Assumption School. For her, my going to school meant one less child to care for in the house, and for me, it meant a world of possible love and attention. In a crisp white blouse and blue jumper, I walked into the classroom with my new lunch pail, a pair of Twinkies, and the *Big-72 Pack of Crayola Crayons, with Built-in Sharpener.* I had arrived!

Immediately, I chose the prettiest blond girl in the class to be my friend. I offered her my Twinkies and Crayolas, but she said, "No! I have one hundred Crayolas, and I don't want to be your friend." Devastated, I started to cry. Through the years, I have come to realize, I have tried over and over to please others in much the same way, instead of looking at my own truth. If I require proof of how early this behavior began, I need only to look at how I held my hands in the kindergarten class picture: both of my thumbs are tucked neatly under my index finger. I was hiding what the thumb itself represents, my will.

Sister Mary Angelis was only nineteen years old at the time, but she saw the truth in class that day. She bent down so that she could look directly into my eyes when she said, "You do not need to bribe someone to be your friend. You, just you, are enough. God loves you, and so do I." When she appeared in the cathedral so many years later, I was in much the same state as I had been in kindergarten, needing to be reminded of my worth. As the sun poured warmth and hope into the moment, we recognized each other. With a few words, Sister Mary Angelis reminded me of that truth.

Finally, there is another kind of truth that people must learn about themselves: their own will, either willingness *or* willfulness, can lead to actions whose consequences they are responsible for.

I received a call from a client named Doris, a public relations person whom I usually read whenever something major happens in her life, from job changes to relationship issues. This time, though, Doris called because she had recommended me to her boss. He was highly skeptical of palmistry and psychics, but since he trusted her, by extension he trusted me.

Raymond was a powerful stockbroker; even the name Trump could be found on his client roster. We arranged a phone appointment, because I am able to work on the phone as well as in person, although without the benefit of touching hands. I simply use my spiritual eye, since a reading is largely a matter of concentrated energy.

My sense of Raymond's situation came immediately. He was depressed and felt that his world was caving in on him. After I said as much, I could hear his sigh of relief. When I told him I saw three children, he said they were his. But I also saw another little boy. Raymond swallowed hard, and I heard a sharp intake of breath. I soon focused on the main reason he had called. Raymond was in legal trouble for tax evasion, and a few years back, his wife had chosen to have an abortion, which was unacceptable to his religion. His wife was planning to enter public office, so there was sure to be some scrutiny into his life. Raymond felt as if he had been pushed against a wall, and he was scared enough to call a psychic, figuring, what did he have to lose?

I knew he had to become willing to take responsibility for his actions. "Own up and pay up," I advised, telling him that facing the truth was the only way to stop a difficult situation from becoming even worse.

Quietly, Raymond said he would. His voice let me know how shaken he was by the reading.

The next day Doris called again. Raymond wanted to meet me in person, so he was going to send his helicopter to pick me up and fly me to New York City. After agreeing on a date and time, I went to our local airport and was escorted by helicopter to lower Manhattan.

In Raymond's expansive windowed office, there were pictures of several famous clients on the walls, even one of the pope. Raymond walked in, an impressive, powerful man. Fifty years old, he was fit and trim and wearing a dark suit.

We sat together on the couch, and I held Raymond's hand. I looked at his thumbs first. Raymond had a powerful, *leader's thumb, angled back* hitchhiker-style. I was not at all surprised. I also saw *chains* and *islands* on his emotional, or *heart*, line, indicating that he had internalized some emotional trauma. From the extent of the markings, it was obvious that he had been doing so for some time. His hands were *cold*, indicating his anxious state, and for someone of his size, his hands were *short*, revealing his probable tendency to act on impulse. The *hard* texture of his entire hand alerted me to his considerable vigor and need for action.

Looking directly at him, I warned him that his situation was, indeed, dire and that he might feel terribly unsettled for some time yet. However, I assured him that as long as he did the right thing, he would not go to jail.

I advised him to "clean up his act" and to spend more time with his children, get himself a reputable CPA, and finally, face the truths about his life and marriage. I asked a difficult question: Had he and his wife aborted the child because they were no longer in love? He did not know. By the time I left, Raymond appeared to be relieved. He was also very aware that he had a lot of soul-searching to do.

Eventually, Raymond paid thousands of dollars in back taxes and vowed to contribute a substantial amount of money each year to day-care centers. After taking responsibility for his own actions, Raymond once again found joy in his marriage, vowed to help his wife's campaign, and he even began thinking about starting a new project, perhaps even writing a book.

As these stories have illustrated, sometimes unwittingly, sometimes unwisely, each client used his or her own will and experienced a variety of outcomes. In every case, however, no matter what the outcome, each individual, after facing the truth of his or her circumstances, made further progress on his or her intuitive path. And so it was willfulness—or willingness—that brought them one step closer to grasping the next chapter's promise: *desire*.

WEEKLY EXERCISE

Using Will to Find the Truth

To begin, sit quietly for a few moments with your hands clasped in your lap. Immediately, you will realize the prominence of your *thumbs,* as they sit atop the indomitable structure you have just created by holding your own hands. Then, start to think of what your life would be like if your will was suddenly stolen from you and you had *no choice* but to be truthful. Would this be a challenge for you? Or are you particularly honest? Would you have any difficulty in complying?

For many, the thought of always telling the truth is unsettling. But whether that is the case for you or not, write down how the idea makes you feel.

Next, write down in a journal a secret you are keeping, any

secret, big or small. Follow this by writing down a few things about you that most people do not know. Make sure some of these things are *positive*.

When you are finished, ask yourself: Were the answers hard, or easy? For many people, answering these questions will be hard. In doing this exercise, what becomes fairly clear is that we have been trained to stay away from revealing truths, especially when they are *negative*. It also becomes clear how hard it is for most of us to reveal *positive* things about ourselves. Secrets, while loaded with dramatic tension in movies, do little for us in our daily lives. When we long for the deep sense of connection that honest communication can yield, keeping secrets from ourselves, and others, inhibits our growth. It also becomes an insidious habit.

During the forthcoming week, be mindful of your *thumbs* as you think about the ideas of will and the truth. Listen to what these concepts mean and how they relate to each other in songs, poetry, literature, film, and mass media. Think about your own will and how it and truth exist in relation to your own life; how the larger, basic truths in life are so easily ignored, such as that the sun rises every morning.

Finally, choose one day this week in which you will tell the truth, no matter what. Use your will wisely and make a pact with a lover or friend if that makes it easier. Be thoughtful and conscientious as the hours pass, and take note of how you feel at the end of the day. What happened? Chances are, you will feel lighter and more free as a result, no matter what the consequences may have been. Your thumb may even noticeably relax. You will also discover that it is easier to tell the truth than you might have thought.

And remember, anything that can be done for a day can be yours for a lifetime.

In my own life, I knew the abusive situation within my childhood home would stay the same until I told the truth about it. At the time, my fists seemed clenched in fear and frustration for good. As my own story illustrates, simply telling the truth does not necessarily change anything, but it is the essential beginning toward realizing just what is and is not acceptable in your life. Only then can we begin to think about the possibility of meaningful and everlasting change.

Today, I still sit in wonder when I look at my own hands. As my fate has unfolded, so, too, have my hands. My closed fists have become open palms, sanctioning me to accept life's gifts and trials with open arms and an open heart.

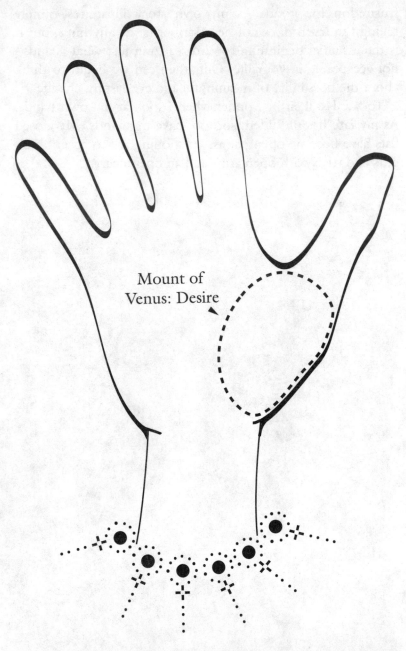

Mount of
Venus: Desire

Find Pleasure and Desire on the Mount of Venus.

EIGHT

Desire: The Mount of Venus

T he hand is comprised not only of its body and fingers, but also the seven *mounts* that can be found across its palm. Each mount provides information relating to the potential of a pérson's character, whereas particular aspects of personality are clearly indicated by the length and shape of individual fingers or the hand's various markings and lines. In traditional palmistry, the mounts are relied on for revealing interests, talents, and potential. The *Mount of Venus* is the most prominent. Found at the base of the thumb, this area of the hand literally supports the thumb's forcefulness. As the thumb's foundation, the Venus mount embodies our *desire*; it is the area of the hand that represents our passion, energy, and desire for affection and harmony. The Mount of Venus provides a bounty of information to us, shedding light on the preconceived attitudes and beliefs we hold that can interfere with realizing our desires. For those of us lucky enough to be conscious of our true desires, this area is well-developed and fleshy, like a ripe, succulent piece of fruit.

111

I once had the opportunity to read the hand of the world's greatest abstract painter, Willem de Kooning. His was the perfect example of desire realized in the flesh: the mount around de Kooning's thumb was thick and full, the flesh a vital, soft pink, indicating a passionate emotional existence. It was the ultimate artist's hand. And though he was well past his prime when we met, his hand was a testimony to his spirit: it was vigorous and youthful, as though the challenges of life and the passage of time had not dimmed his passions at all.

Named after the goddess of love, the mount of Venus reveals our capacity for love, just as it shows our relationship to desire and creativity, the vital forces that allow us to experience love.

As the goddess of love and beauty, Aphrodite/Venus held great power over both mortals and immortals. It should come as no surprise, then, that she is featured in numerous myths, poems, and plays, though not always because of her success at love. Some of the most compelling myths deal with the consequences the goddess herself suffered as a result of being the victim of love. The story of Aphrodite and her bittersweet interlude with Adonis, a mere human being, is an interesting study of the double-edged sword that passion can be. In this myth, the emergence of vulnerability is brought forth by the idea that even the gods could suffer over love and so were certainly not immune to the pains and passions that we humans experience.

Finally, the legacy of Venus reminds us that tenderness and impulsiveness, as well as a desire for affection and harmony, can enrich our lives, and that comfort and even luxury are desirable and should be honored and sought in our lives.

"Doors will open where you didn't know they were going to be," wrote professor Joseph Campbell in *The Power of Myth*. What that idea suggests is that once we allow ourselves to follow our "bliss"—that is, acknowledge our passions and our heart's true desires—doors that we did not even know existed will open.

The ideas of Dr. Deepak Chopra are quite similar to Campbell's on this concept when he suggests that we "let the universe handle the details. Your intentions and desires, when released in the gap, have infinite organizing power." The "gap" Chopra cites is simply that silent space between thoughts, the place where our desires grow and blossom, where we exist in our most essential state. The goal, then, is to allow ourselves to acknowledge our desires and allow them to take us to places we can now only imagine.

Take a moment now to consider the Venus mount on your own hand. If you have a *high, firm* mount, you have probably never doubted for a moment that you can do anything you set out to do, for you have the energy to work all day and dance into the night. Love and dance you might, for a love of music and creativity is also associated with this mount.

For those of you with a *soft, flat* mount, you are apt to observe life closely, and because you have taken the time to become aware of yourself and the world around you, others have something to learn from you. You may, however, benefit by increasing your physical activity, and by doing so, you will develop a larger capacity for *fun,* which is an often overlooked and undervalued characteristic of passionate living. As you begin to discover and know your very unique, expressive, and passionate self, you will actually see the Mount of Venus develop and change on your own hand.

When the mount is *overdeveloped,* however, it may reveal a hot temperament and the possible tendency to allow impulsiveness and sensuality to overwhelm your life. In the heat of passion, you may say yes rather than no for the sake of the moment, rather than as a true expression of your feelings. You may also become a "shop till you drop" type, overspending without even realizing it, or drive yourself into workaholism. A tendency toward extremes is inherent.

An *underdeveloped* mount indicates that you are the type of person who chooses reason over impulse. Depending on the situation, this may work against your overall vitality, causing you to miss opportunities for professional success, in love and relationships, and the simple joys and pleasures of daily living. You may be so programmed to "follow the rules" and "live by the book" that the unique and life-giving opportunities that are born of spontaneity may pass you by. This manifests itself as a tendency to worry about the future, rather than focusing on the present.

There are many other markings that may appear on the Venus mount, but these are relatively transient. As previously discussed, we are born with three principal lines in our hands, the *life, heart,* and *head* lines. While these markings display immutable aspects of personality and will most likely remain the same, many other finer lines, patterns, and marks will just as surely change along with aspects of your life, your circumstances, and your personality.

If there is a single *star* on your Venus mount, for example, it indicates that you are undergoing or have undergone an important experience related to love. It may also mean that you are liable to be deceived by a friend. You should read this sign as a blessing and take the opportunity to step back, assess your relationships, and be mindful of your own heart and feelings.

If there is a *square* in the area, the possibilities are again twofold: the square may be a positive sign, signaling a feeling of overall security on your part, or it may represent the existence of an unresolved problem that you need to address. The discovery of such a mark, is, again, a great opportunity for you to stop and focus on what is blocking your life. It is yet another opportunity to gain self-knowledge and make necessary changes in your life. If you do so honestly and with an open heart, the square will surely fade from your hand.

Possessing a *grille* on your mount indicates that you are a person of abundant lust, and your consuming sexuality may in fact influence the direction your life takes for extended periods of time. Grilles, too, are typical of those who heighten their sexuality with fantasies. This use of imagination is not surprising, for grilles indicate a capacity for creativity and artistic flair.

Those of you with *vertical lines* in this area experience a balanced and healthy sexuality, and though passionate, you don't get carried away. These vertical lines also reveal an ability to approach life in a well-rounded manner and that there is a true respect for instinct and intuition present. *Single bar lines* in this area indicate challenges with affection, love, and physical passion; other concerns, such as career matters, may take precedence. Similarly, *horizontal lines* indicate that you have obstacles that prevent you from fulfilling the promise of Venus. Those with horizontal lines may be inhibited or hampered by adhering to a strict (and restrictive) code of morality.

When I look at my own hand, I am pleased to see a well-developed Venus mount, which depicts my desire for a loving family. While this is certainly a reflection of my personality, I also have some *horizontal lines* in this area, indicating the struggles I have had to overcome to realize my passionate potential and create my loving family. Years ago, I used to pray that I would know when the man I was destined to love would come into my life. Abundant in innocence and lacking in self-knowledge, I had so little clarity in my youth about how I might actually realize this dream. In romantic relationships, I continually chose abusive men, but I dedicated myself to breaking this pattern and finding healthier ways to relate to men, and over the years, I've seen the lines recede and the shape of my Mount of Venus change. Now, only a single *cross* appears on my mount, which keeps me constantly aware of my most deeply felt passion, my need for a healthy and loving primary relationship—my marriage.

Remember the lovely Miss Augustine I met on the bus when I was eight? When I saw her again, after I had grown my nails, she took my hand to admire my nails, and asked me if I had cut myself, for there, on the fleshy part of my palm, the Venus mount, I had quite unconsciously begun to dig my newly grown nails into the soft flesh, creating a number of deep horizontal indentations.

When single, horizontal markings appear on that mount, I learned many years later, it is a clear indicator that there are obstacles or challenges that need to be addressed before you can truly be fulfilled in love. Years later, I possess the clarity to see that in my case, those marks were an accurate, early expression of my continued but often thwarted *desire* to have the kind of happy home life I now enjoy and cherish.

Regardless of the type of Venus mount you presently have, this area of the hand reveals information about many different types of desires. This line from Proverbs advises us that, "the desire accomplished is sweet to the soul," an idea that is echoed in the work of many of our greatest thinkers. The author Samuel Johnson believed that "Some desire is necessary to keep life in motion," while philosopher and psychologist William James wrote, "If you care enough for a result, you will most certainly attain it." The critic John Ruskin, always an independent thinker, had his own spin on this concept: "Tell me what you like and I'll tell you what you are." A breath away is this thought of Mark Twain's: "I can teach anybody how to get what they want out of life. The problem is that I can't find anybody who can tell me what they want." Whether we do or do not know what our desires are, the fact remains that until we come to know ourselves deeply and fully, desire itself moves through us in an enormously complex, often misunderstood manner, and we must often overcome enormous obstacles, within as well as without, to fulfill our heart's desire.

These ideas remind me of a story I heard about an old man who one day found a silky cocoon in the woods. This was a man who spent his life loving things many people despised—insects. Having never seen a cocoon quite like this one, he decided to take it home and watch it develop into a butterfly. He gently placed the cocoon on his kitchen table and watched it for nearly a week. On the seventh day, the cocoon started to move. In a few moments, it moved frantically. The old man felt sorry for the little butterfly inside the cocoon as he watched it struggle and struggle.

Desiring only to help the butterfly, the old man took a surgical scalpel and gently slit the cocoon open so that the butterfly could emerge. One small slice was all it took for the butterfly to break free from its cocoon. It emerged, flexed its wings, flew up into the air, then fell to the floor motionless. The old man did not know what to do or think. Had he accidentally killed the little butterfly? No, it was still moving a bit, but as it moved, the old man noticed that the butterfly lacked any of the beautiful colors and designs that distinguish butterflies from mere moths. He was dumbfounded and quite perplexed, eventually deciding that the best thing to do for the butterfly was to place it gently back into its cocoon.

The old man placed a drop of honey on the cocoon in order to seal it once he had gently placed the butterfly inside, leaving the butterfly to nestle in its natural state. The next day, he noticed that the cocoon was moving again and that the butterfly was struggling and struggling once more. After many hours, the butterfly broke free of its cocoon and stretched its wings. Its wings were now radiant with stunning colors and designs. After a moment, the butterfly lifted itself into the air and flew out of the window. The old man was overjoyed. Yet, he still pondered what went wrong when he had opened the cocoon only a day earlier.

He went to the library and read everything he could find about butterflies and cocoons. Book after book said nothing that helped. Finally, he found the answer. The butterfly *must* struggle within the cocoon in order to eventually become whole and beautiful. As if divinely designed, its beauty and grace followed only after its obstacles had been overcome. As for the man, we can see that his own desire made him impatient; he acted in haste and, in doing so, nearly lost the chance to witness the butterfly's natural beauty.

This story illustrates what I have witnessed time and again in my own life and in the lives of my clients. Struggle is part of the process of realizing our desires. The lesson within this simple story is also simple. Once we accept that we will struggle as we grow, we, too, will one day fly as effortlessly and gracefully as the butterfly.

Quite often, that lesson is painfully learned. Lucy is a forty-five-year-old, high-powered cosmetics executive. She is a tall, blond, beautifully composed professional who commands a six-figure salary. From all appearances, it seems that Lucy has it all. During her initial consultation with me, however, she expressed anxiety about where her life was headed. She was deeply sad over the fact that she had never been married, and her greatest regret was that she had never had a child. Lucy had *large* hands, which told me that she gravitated toward the small details in life. I then noticed her *heart* line and saw that it was deep and clear, which indicated that she did indeed have the ability to attract a suitable mate. When I felt her *Mount of Venus,* though, I found this area hard and unflexible, indicating just that, an inflexibility that would block the fulfillment of desire. When I questioned her about her goals, Lucy admitted that she felt it was too late for her to have those things she most wanted, that she was past her prime and that she truly believed that she was too old to find her mate and certainly too old to have a child. Yet her mount, which was *high* and *firm,* indicated that her passion, though dormant, was still alive. As Lucy revealed certain aspects of her experiences and behavior, it became clear that underlying her outward appearance of success, she suffered from a deeply rooted insecurity that lay in her belief that she was, in her own words, "not special enough." Her confession did not surprise me, for I have observed a similar kind of insecurity in many successful businesswomen who want it all but deep down inside believe they do not deserve it.

In addition to the unyielding surface of Lucy's mount, *crosses* covered the area, denoting a confused or complicated love life. Lucy admitted that she had frequently become involved with unavailable men, some of whom were even married. She had a tendency to start affairs while vacationing and then abandon them when she returned to the work world.

Using her own hand as a map, I pointed out that her true destiny lay right there and that all she needed to do was honor that truth with the deepest self-love and respect she could muster. In the area of the hand that indicates if children will enter someone's life (the vertical lines that appear to the side of the palm beneath the pinky finger), I saw three lines. Lucy admitted she had had two abortions. "But there's a third line," I offered. "You have another chance to have a baby!" In the area of the hand that is specific to relationships or marriage (in the same area beneath the pinky), I saw several horizontal lines. "Your love life is far from over," I assured her. But whether Lucy could truly grasp the truth her hand revealed was up to her. She was being called upon, she realized, to dispel the terrible (and false) belief that she was not special enough to have everything life offered. Lucy called me after a few months of painful soul-searching. She was now having a wonderful affair (with an unmarried and emotionally available man) and had just found out she was pregnant. Though she ultimately chose not to remain with that particular man, Lucy now has an adorable three-year-old boy and a long-standing, healthy relationship with another man who is deeply committed to Lucy and her son.

Loretta's story is another that illustrates the complexity involved in realizing our desires. A therapist client of mine suggested that Loretta, his personal trainer, come to see me when she'd reached a very low point in her life. Through Ted, I learned that Loretta was quite closed to the idea of seeing me until Ted told her that I might be able to contact her parents, who had been killed in a plane crash not long before.

I told Ted that though some psychics specialize in contacting those who have passed on from this world to the next, I am not one of those. I prefer, instead, to focus on the living. While it is true that I have received messages from those across the mundane divide, I do not usually seek that connection during a reading.

In the end, Loretta surprised us both and called to make an appointment. She was a beautiful, fit woman in her late twenties. Her *small* hands immediately revealed her sensitive and lively nature, while their *narrowness* spoke of her fearfulness, not an unusual combination. Her *Mount of Venus* was somewhat *underdeveloped,* letting me know that she was the type of person who usually relied heavily on reason over impulse.

As the reading progressed, I was not surprised, then, to hear that Loretta's life had been carefully mapped out, with the help of her parents. She had attended the right schools, had the right friends. Personal training was a mere hobby while she decided between a law or other professional career. She had been in no hurry to decide what to do with her life when her parents were killed in a plane crash and Loretta's life "just fell apart."

She began to question life in general and did not see how she could live a meaningful existence, explaining that her boyfriend had broken up with her just days before her parents died and that for the first time in her life, Loretta was really alone. Because she had been born late in her parents' life, she was an only child. "As if that isn't bad enough," Loretta told me, "look at my hair! It's gone!" She pulled off her hat then, so that I could see the mere wisps of hair that covered her head. (I advised her to see a dermatologist who, I assured her, would explain that the loss of her hair was a stress reaction and that it would surely grow back.)

Loretta told me then that her hair didn't matter anymore, because her life didn't. She had fallen into a deep depression. The only thing keeping her afloat, I soon found out, was a stray kitten she had found. Here was a tiny helpless animal that needed care, and Loretta could provide it. The reason she had come to see me, she stated, was to ask about suicide. She wanted to know what would happen if she killed herself. Would she come back and meet the same people all over again?

I explained that we come into this life with a *sacred contract*, that our souls plan in advance the lives we will lead, and that for those of us who commit suicide, we come back right away and without the benefit of planning the lessons that are part of the divine plan God has designed for us. I warned her that suicide was indeed a dangerous act, because those who ended their lives were destined to repeat what they were running away from. "Oh, no," she said. "You mean I might come back without any hair at all?"

I was glad to laugh with her and chose that moment of openness to begin our reading. As I took her hand, I saw the *break* in her *life* line, also marked by an *island*, indicating the shock and loss she had experienced. I also saw a *clear, deep head* line, indicating her intellectual promise. Too, I saw the many *chains* that covered her *heart* line, revealing that love was the most challenging area of her life. Finally, I noticed her *Mount of Venus*, which was *overdeveloped*, indicating a hot temperament. Chances were, before me was a person who did not remain satisfied for long periods of time.

From the moment Loretta sat down, it was clear that she had lost her desire to live fully engaged in her life, for she had suffered too much loss in a deeply shocking way. How would I get through to her that I saw the promise in her own hand, that she could realize her dreams? I thought of the kitten she had mentioned and how she herself was like the poor little creature—abandoned and lost, with nobody to love and comfort her. I expressed the correlation I saw between the two and pointed out that although Loretta was currently in a state of despair, not yet fully grieving over the losses she had experienced, she was still able to love and cherish the tiny precious life of the kitten. By comforting another living creature, she would find her way to loving herself: the proof was right there in front of her.

Loretta became very emotional as our session ended. She was as confused about her life as ever, she said, but what I said had made some sense. I later learned that she became very involved in our local animal rescue center and, more recently, has joined up with a group that provides aid for the many Albanian refugee children who have lost their parents in that devastating war. Her deep desire to live a meaningful life has indeed been realized, and I have no doubt that Loretta will find much love, comfort, and companionship in the future: she will not be alone.

Sometimes it takes what we consider "terrible" circumstances or tragic events to jolt us into a state that forces us to do the hard work to get closer to our true and authentic selves. At other moments, as Dr. Deepak Chopra points out, "the right mix of matter, energy, and space-time events creates whatever it is that you desire." Or, more simply, things just seem to fall into place, almost by magic. This is an idea I agree with wholeheartedly. A few autumns ago, I met a lovely young woman of twenty-one when I returned to East Hampton after a trip to New York City. We sat next to each other on the bus, engaging in small talk about the weather and the upcoming weekend, which featured the increasingly popular and chic Hamptons Film Festival. The previous year, Steven Spielberg had spoken at the festival, and my bus mate, Linda, was excited about the possibility of being discovered by him or another famous director. Linda longed to be an actress. A plump, blond-haired, blue-eyed bundle of vivacious energy, she had just moved to the city after finishing college in the Midwest, where she had grown up. She asked me what I did for a living, and when I told her I was a palmist and a psychic she became even more excited.

As I looked out the window at the colorful foliage on the trees, I remembered how much the attention Miss Augustine had given me had meant, and I offered to look at Linda's hands, which were *hot, soft,* and *fleshy.* Immediately, I knew that Linda was someone who expressed her feelings openly, if not exaggeratedly, and was therefore well-suited for the theater. She was also a dreamer with a deep desire for material possessions. Linda's *Mount of Venus* was *overdeveloped* and marked by a *cross.* This indicated that Linda was not only highly sensual, but that there would likely be periods in her life when a potentially unhealthy and consuming sexuality might dominate her life. There were also some *chains* on both her *heart* and *head* lines, indicating obstacles that I sensed were in competition with each other.

"Linda," I began, "you are torn about your boyfriend back home and your career in New York, aren't you?" "How did you know that?" she asked, and I showed her the lines on her hand. "What should I do?" she pressed, and of course, I stressed that the choices to be made were hers alone. "Your desire for love is as strong as your desire to act. It's up to you to decide whether marrying your boyfriend is what you want to do. If you do go home," I continued, "you *will* marry him, which will allow you the chance to get to know yourself better before venturing out into the theater world. That means your acting, as well as the rest of your life, will be richer as a result of your insight."

Following our bus ride, Linda began sending me postcards

from time to time. Not long after we met, she did indeed return home and she married her young man. She hoped to come back to New York someday and fulfill her heart's desire in the theater, but in the meantime, her desire for love had taken center stage.

While the promise of love exists in every hand, the capacity to realize our desires can become hidden beneath deeply rooted fears. The poet Goethe even believed that "Man errs as long as he strives." I tend to accept the wisdom of a Gaelic proverb more readily: "More than we use is more than we want." Regardless, the experience of painful life occurrences, such as devastating loss or disappointment, may find us retreating into familiar, albeit unsatisfying, patterns. It is then that our desires may become blocked without our even knowing it, and our Venus mount may become flat and hard.

When I first met with Margaret, a slender woman in her sixties, I saw a great sadness in her eyes. Taking both of her *small* hands in mine, I found them *limp* and *clammy,* a clear indicator of how disturbed she was. Her hands were also oval-shaped, which often indicates strong sexual magnetism. A cold chill ran down my leg as I studied Margaret's right hand, which was marked with several *islands* and a significant *red dot* on her *Mount of Venus* that nearly crossed her *life* line. A dot this pronounced and in this area marks a sudden shock in life, and the presence of the islands, generally speaking, often indicates depression. Margaret's Mount of Venus was *soft* and *fleshy,* indicating a strong sexual drive, and it was set high on her hand (like Mr. de Kooning's), indicating an ability to experience life passionately. Margaret, it was clear, was being pulled in many directions. When I told her I knew she was depressed because of the death of a loved one, she began to weep. Her son had died of a drug overdose just a year before, and she was determined to prevent her daughter-in-law from inheriting his trust fund. A glance at her *Jupiter* (or *index*) finger, which leaned toward the middle finger, told me she had financial issues. At the very least, this showed that she worried about her finances unnecessarily. I sensed that Margaret's focus on money and on her son's trust fund formed a much-needed diversion from something else, and that the true source of her misery lay elsewhere.

When I mentioned sex and passion, I hit a chord with her, which was not surprising: most people respond very strongly to this subject. The reading revealed that Margaret had lost not only her passion for sex, but her very passion for life and art, her deepest desires. "I stopped painting," she revealed, the thing she loved more than any other. When I asked Margaret to consider dropping her battles with lawyers over the trust fund—it would not bring back her son, after all—and concentrate instead on releasing some of her sadness in her painting, her expression brightened as if a cloud had lifted. If she were to surrender to her grief, rather than mask it with misplaced anger, I was sure her love life would regain its passion. By the time Margaret left, the sadness in her eyes was replaced with a new spark. She called soon after our initial meeting to invite me to her studio. She wanted to show me a painting she had begun, one that she hoped would celebrate the spirit of her beloved son.

Awareness itself is a gift. What I gained from meeting with Margaret was the uplifting awareness that it is only when we reveal our own truths that we may begin to remove the barriers or change the patterns that prevent us from experiencing desire. Once we remove these blocks, our creativity is released and freed and desire can flourish. We need only look at one of Mr. de Kooning's paintings to see the truth in this.

All of the examples I've used so far illustrate how challenging and even heroic overcoming the obstacles to true desire can be. Yet desire, like clarity itself, may also surprise us with its sudden, often unexpected arrival. And these are moments of grace. At these times, we are often blessed with an abundance of exquisite awareness.

Years ago, I worked as a palmist in a club on Manhattan's Upper East Side. One evening was especially uneventful until a tall, handsome man with sparkling gray eyes and Tom Selleck dimples arrived. He came directly to my table and asked that I read his hand. I first noticed that his *head* line sloped downward and said, "I see that you are a writer." He replied, "Yes, I studied journalism at Columbia University." When I saw how his *head* and *heart* lines connected just a bit, I said it was clear that he had strong loyalties to his family and friends, and he told me he lived just two blocks away from his elderly parents' apartment. Then I felt his well-defined Venus mount, took a deep breath, and blurted out, "You are going to marry me!" Without missing a beat, he said, "Well, if I am going to marry you, maybe we should have dinner tonight."

I was shocked that those words had spilled from my mouth, and when the stranger replied so charmingly, a warm feeling of comfort and well-being flowed through my entire being, an undeniable manifestation of my own *desire*. Smiling, he told me that he had never been to this nightclub before, but that he had just been walking along Fifty-fourth Street and had been inexplicably drawn into the building.

At that moment, I was struck with complete clarity: I knew that I would love this man. We went to dinner in Chinatown and held hands the entire time. It was such a pure, loving feeling. I let go of his hand only long enough to crack open a fortune cookie. "There is a true and sincere friendship between you," it read. Now, after seventeen years of marriage to this man, I can honestly say I held my fate in my hands in that Chinese restaurant so many years before. And I still take every opportunity to hold this man's hand today.

What is so significant to me about this story is that had I relied on reason and logic instead of my own instinctive feelings of certainty and desire, chances are my husband would have been just another client.

WEEKLY EXERCISE

Creating a Desire Map

What exactly is *desire*? It is the very foundation of who each of us is, and for each of us, our desires are unique and precious. In simple terms, desire is the ability to long for, to hope for, or to wish for something. It sounds so simple, and yet, for many of us, our true desires are hidden in the shadows of ourselves, just out of reach. Perhaps we cling too closely to a notion once voiced by Socrates: "The fewer our wants the more we resemble the gods." For those of us who have forgotten that desire is an essential aspect of who we are, this biblical proverb may ring all too true: "First deserve, then desire." On this point, I beg to part company with these philosophies and boldly state that desire leads to freedom, and without desire, like a plant without water, our souls wither, unable to blossom and grow.

This week, we will continue to enlighten our everyday experiences by utilizing our journals. As the exercises of the last chapter revealed, truth is the very foundation for growth. Desire, then, is the first step toward realizing our dreams. To better understand our goals and dreams, we first need to

expose the barriers that prevent us from experiencing fulfillment and satisfaction.

Take a moment now to identify what barriers or promises
exist on your own Venus mount. Include any additional
information about the presence of rashes, warts, or cuts. This
is your *Desire Map*. By seeing and identifying those markings
on the area of the hand that houses desire, you will be able to
identify which desires lie unfulfilled and what promises lie
ahead.

Next, write a paragraph that explicitly describes your
desires and goals. Most important, write what you want *as if
it has already happened*. For example, if you are a person for
whom physical illness often manifests as a result of stress,
write something like, "My body is healthy and I never get
sick." Other examples may have something to do with desire
itself, as in, "I see life clearly" or "I am deeply intuitive." You
may wish to focus on personal or professional issues: "I am
happy in my career," or "My relationship with my significant
other is loving and respectful." Whatever the actual desire is,
claim it as if it is already so, for that is how a Desire Map
becomes your essential means for changing negative patterns
in your life.

After you have identified your desires on paper, match
those ideas with mental *pictures*. Literally, close your eyes
and begin to *see* your fully realized desires. An easy, fun
way to approach this aspect of inner consciousness is to
create a collage of desires. Fill some pages in your journal
with actual pictures that you clip from magazines or photo
albums, or because the Venus mount promises creativity,
you may wish to draw or paint your own. Include pictures
of your family, your loving mate, your healthy body, whatever you desire. As you commit these images to paper, you
are also committing yourself to attaining them by taking an
action to transform the barriers that may presently inhibit
aspects of your experience. This week, add to these pages

as often as you can, and feel free, as you go deeper into the following chapters, to return and add to your Desire Map whenever new goals or desires manifest themselves. You will be amazed at how various marks change and sometimes disappear as you change.

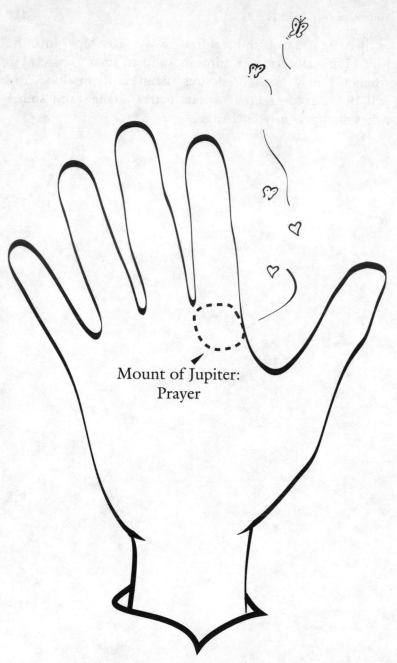

Mount of Jupiter:
Prayer

*A Longing for Spirituality and Prayer
Is Revealed by the Mount of Jupiter.*

NINE

Prayer: The Mount of Jupiter

The area of the hand that indicates our longing for guidance from some kind of deity or spiritual source is the *Mount of Jupiter*. It is located between the *head* and *heart* lines and directly beneath the *index* (or *Jupiter*) finger. Even if we do not know it, this is the part of our hand that invites our belief in a spiritual power greater than ourselves; or, at the very least, it is the area that indicates our willingness to believe in miracles.

By the time Christ was born, many cultures had relied on palmistry for hundreds of years as part of mankind's natural and innate quest to find a deeper meaning for our existence. Prayer, often misunderstood by so many, is so powerful as to be nearly if not fully miraculous in our lives. Of the seven mounts on the human hand, the *Mount of Jupiter* is the one that alerts us to our longing for spirituality. Those of us who believe we have no room within for a connection to God or a higher power, may find that success and achievement come with their own price, a certain hollowness. To banish this hollowness, we must be willing to acknowledge the existence of a spiritual force greater than ourselves. Only then can we experience a true sense of satisfaction and find true freedom. As Christ's words remind us, "So I tell you, whatever you ask for in prayer, believe that you have received it, and it will be yours."

If your Jupiter mount is *well-developed,* you are a spiritually oriented person who has faith that a benevolent power greater than yourself ensures that the universe is brimming with love and abundance, and you derive a great degree of comfort from this belief. If your mount is *overdeveloped,* you may be overly reliant on reason and the realities of the material world, rather than on the spirit. An *average* mount indicates a well-balanced character and a willingness to experience the spiritual world.

If a *grille* covers the Mount of Jupiter, take notice and begin to pray for clarity, for you have a tendency toward mental disorganization and experience the kind of mental confusion that can be alleviated only by prayer. A *star* on the mount is a favorable sign, revealing a healthy spirituality and a go-getter type of personality. More than one star, however, may indicate that the bearer may overlook spiritual values in the race toward success. If you have stars in this area, pray for patience and work to cultivate a sense of gratitude for the bounty and gifts in your life.

Crosses on the Mount of Jupiter indicate that you already possess or have the ability to attract people who bring further abundance into your life. *Chains,* on the other hand, are characteristic of people who complicate their lives with anxieties and fears and lack the spiritual orientation to believe that those around them (including a loving higher power) will bring abundance to their lives. Those with this characteristic should pray for greater openness, which will relieve their anxiety. You will then find that in prayer and stillness, you will surely survive even the most challenging situations. Finally, *circles* reveal a perfectionistic tendency. People with circles on their Jupiter mounts believe that they must be perfect or godlike just to measure up. The irony in this false belief rests in the fact that perfectionists forget that God created man in his image and that we are perfect, in our beautifully "flawed" ways. Those with circles on their Jupiter mounts should pray for a more nonjudgmental mind, especially in regard to themselves.

Regardless of the actual markings you possess, you need only put your hands together and pray for guidance to bring remarkable changes into your life. Whether we know it or not, we are all one as we strive toward higher ground. Each of us is on a path to become the best we can be, here on earth to give of our individual gifts for the greater good of humanity.

Ernest Hemingway is one individual who gave of his talents for the good of man; he is one of the twentieth century's greatest writers. His attitude toward prayer and spirituality, however, can be summed up in what is believed to be his own reworking of a well-known prayer which in this unenlightened version begins: "Our nada who art in nada, nada be thy name . . ."

While we might look on this revision in a humorous light, the sad truth is that Mr. Hemingway—in spite of fame, fortune, and such divinely inspired talent—committed suicide. I firmly believe that this desperate act always reveals a state of spiritual bankruptcy and a sadly sure lack of belief in the power of prayer.

I was once asked to perform stand-up comedy at a local benefit for a fisherman who had suffered a terrible car accident. I nervously agreed. At the time, I had been away from the stage for twenty years. While I practiced my routine, I also prayed. The night of the performance, my stomach began churning with stage fright. To calm myself, I called a prayer line, where operators sat at the ready to pray with callers twenty-four hours a day.

I had called this organization in the past, and each time I made contact I felt as though I had reached a living angel on the other end of the line. When I called this time, the woman answered softly, "How can I pray with you?" I began to tell her my story about going onstage to perform after a hiatus of twenty years. When she said, "Tell me some jokes," I was taken aback. It was hard to believe that this soft-spoken spiritual guide wanted me to do my shtick!

I panicked, but the angel pressed me good-naturedly until I surrendered. She laughed as I told my first few jokes, and I began to calm down. "God has a sense of humor too," she said, "and when we laugh we make the angels happy." With those thoughts in mind, I felt confident that I would not be alone on the stage that night: the angels would be with me. I would like to say that I killed the audience that evening, but the hall was overcrowded and the sound system terrible. I did my best, however, and I heard more than a few angels laughing that night.

Mahatma Gandhi expressed the absolute relevance of prayer so simply and perfectly: "Let everyone try and find that as a result of daily prayer he adds something new to his life, something with which nothing can be compared." I have found this to be an undeniable truth in my own life, and my greatest wish is that you discover its truth in yours.

Quite often, far from seeing prayer as adding something new and beneficial to life, people stumble upon prayer only when they feel there is no other recourse or when they are faced with a significant life crisis of some kind.

I recently read a Swedish client named Eve, a very depressed middle-aged gardener who told me, "I believe in nature," rather than God. Her *life* and *head* lines were connected by *chains,* which is characteristic of those who complicate their lives with unnecessary anxieties and fears. It was clear to me that Eve's closed-minded attitude that life was a landscape of drought was exactly what held her back from happiness. Life, in my experience, is like the opening of a flower, sometimes tightly closed, but eventually blooming and bountiful. I asked Eve whether she might not still be able to till the earth during a drought or plant some bulbs or simply rest before the rain returned, as it always does, to bring harvest and bounty. Her narrow-eyed, disbelieving response said more than words ever could. Eve was not yet ready to look at life as a growing, blossoming promise, and so I merely counseled her to beware of all the missed opportunities she experienced because of her limited beliefs. I told her that an openness to a new sense of spirituality would free her to experience more of life's bounty and joy.

I have yet to hear from Eve again, but the irony of her circumstances, that she was a gardener named Eve, has kept me ever mindful of the original Eve's part in Genesis, the first chapter of the Bible, in which she, too, refuses to listen to another's beliefs.

I have met many clients who, initially, are as disbelieving as Eve, and at times, I have been blessed with the opportunity to witness the transformation of those beliefs. One such client was a gentleman who called my television show to ask about my work with the police department. I replied simply that I had worked with the police. The caller then asked if the police called me or I called them. It didn't take a psychic to know that something was perhaps seriously amiss in the caller's world, and I responded to the question by telling him that I regarded this as a confidential matter and was therefore not at liberty to discuss it further. I then suggested that he write to me if he wished to set up a phone appointment, since many callers do not live nearby.

The following day, I received Barry's letter, which he had sent by overnight mail. Though he lived several hours away, he wanted to set up a face-to-face meeting as soon as possible. The tone of his letter was very impatient, and I could sense its underlying desperation, so I agreed. A week later, Barry arrived at my office. He was a big-framed, intense man whose "wise guy" energy neither surprised nor intimidated me. I expected it. After I told him a few things about his life, including the fact that his father had deserted the family when Barry was fourteen and that Barry had gone on to support his mother and brother, I gained his trust and he sat down.

Even though I "just knew" why he had come to see me, I sat quietly as he told me that his wife wanted a divorce. She was the keeper of many secrets, according to Barry, and in anger had threatened to divulge them to certain "authorities," if he did not comply with her wishes in the divorce proceedings. Communication had broken down between the couple, and the situation seemed hopeless.

Barry implied that he always got what he wanted, no matter what it took. And although he was an intimidating presence, I was not fearful; I sensed that beneath the surface he felt out of control, deeply sad, and that he had no idea how to put these emotions into words, which isolated him even further. I reached for Barry's hand and saw the proof of what I had already intuited. His hands were *short* and *hard,* and crossed by a *Simian line.* On his dominant hand only, his *thumb* had a *clubbed tip.* Barry could be an impatient, disorganized, even thoughtless, individual, largely unwilling to compromise. The Simian line indicated his intense energy and that his behavior was unpredictable when he was angry. His thumb expressed his impatience and a tendency to avoid the truth. Finally, his *Mount of Jupiter* was covered by a *grille,* indicating a personality prone to confusion and indecision.

Underneath the hard shell of this person was an individual who was scared of losing his family and so was trying to act as tough as he could. No wilting lily myself, I was blunt with

Barry, telling him that he needed to take responsibility for his own actions and stop endangering his family with illegal activities. Barry was quiet then, asking if his wife would take him back. "Not right now. Not until you change your attitude and your line of work." "Are you crazy? You mean she's not going to let me back in the house? There is no way she or anyone's going to tell me what to do . . ."

I simply told Barry that if he tried to go home and if he ever laid a hand on his wife, he would end up in jail. Somehow, Barry heard my words and calmed down. "What can I do?" he asked softly. "You can begin to pray. Start praying to God to help you find a new direction for your life." I also suggested that he find a stress therapist to help him with his enormous anger. Before he left, I gave him the number of the prayer hot line, stating my belief that miracles can happen when two or more people pray about something together.

Almost a year later, Barry called again. After he had gone back to school to become an accountant, his wife had called off the divorce and taken him back. In a gentle voice, Barry thanked me for helping him discover the miracle of prayer.

Just over a year ago, Ethan, an English gentleman in his early thirties came to me for a reading because he was struggling with a business decision. At the time, Ethan had a prosperous business in English landscape design. Merely by touching his hands, it came to me that he was in the States for just a short time. "You're just visiting?" I asked. Ethan nodded. The flesh of his palm was smooth and his fingers were long, denoting sensitivity and a love of beauty. "More like an artist than a gardener," I said, and Ethan admitted he was. His hands were *square*, which told me that Ethan was a very hard worker. I noticed that his *heart* line had several *descending branches* and *islands*, and so I knew that he had

had his share of major depressions and disappointments. The downward angle of one branch alerted me to the fact that Ethan was hesitant to discuss a current emotional situation. On his *Mount of Jupiter, chains* spread, indicating that his health was becoming affected by his worried mental state. "You are upset in a relationship, and you feel helpless about solving it," I said.

Ethan again nodded. "Yes, there's a girl. I followed her here last year." "But the relationship is now over," I said softly. Ethan sadly nodded. Though he had wanted to consult with me about his career, I felt the relationship was the real reason he had come to see me, since it was preventing him from moving forward in his life. "Your girlfriend is seeing someone else, and you are feeling depressed. You want to leave everything you have created here and say good-bye to this country altogether. At this point, you are angry that you left your life behind and came here at all," I said. "Also, I see twins. Did you leave them behind in England?"

"How do you know all this?!" Ethan demanded. I showed him the lines of his own hand, how the depression and sadness was affecting every area of his life, and exactly where the information about his children lay. And I could simply intuit the truth of his circumstances. "What should I do?" he asked plaintively. "The answers are inside of you. Pray, and you will know what to do. Think of planting a garden. In time, the seeds will grow." Ethan stared at me. I knew that his anger and depression would melt away if he could pray *for* his ex-girlfriend and for himself. "Listen to your heart. Trust the answers that come from prayer; they will be there, Ethan."

Ethan was pale. "My father was a minister, and that is exactly what he would say to me. He died just before I left England. Were you feeling his spirit?" I shook my head. "I was feeling yours," I said. I knew that if he prayed he would eventually see the bigger picture of his life and be able to look inward for his own answers. Soon he would forgive his ex-girlfriend for leaving him, and he would return to his twin boys, three years old now, back in England.

Several months later, I received a postcard from London. Ethan had prayed, he wrote. He had returned home and opened a thriving landscape design business nearby. He was thrilled to be close to his sons again. So much more open and willing than Eve, Ethan had replanted the garden of his life, and it was now blooming.

Prayer, however, is not always about situations we want or need to create. Sometimes, prayer is about what already exists, and we just do not know it. Cassandra, a thirty-seven-year-old single mother, is fiercely talented in many areas. She is also quite beautiful, with finely chiseled features and remarkably bright eyes that dazzle with life. Cassandra and I traded talents one day; she did some faux finishing at my house in exchange for a reading. One look at her hand told me more than she ever could, for Cassandra's Jupiter mount was marked with *crosses* and *stars*. Here was a person who could visualize or pray for something, and it would happen. I questioned whether Cassandra was aware of this. "Well," she answered, "I told a friend of mine recently that I am ready to date now, but that I didn't want to look for a man. I wanted him to come and find me. I even prayed about it."

A few days later, a man knocked on her door, a big, sexy guy who looked like a model from a romance book jacket. "He had seen me around, and he came over to ask me out." Amazing as this may sound, Cassandra's palm revealed the rest of the story. There were wide spaces between her fingers, indicating her sense of adventure and a certain fearlessness in the face of conventionality. Her hands' *oval* shape revealed her sensual nature. Her *heart* line went straight across her hand, indicating that her mind worked in a masculine rather than feminine way; that is to say, she kept tight control of her emotions, unwilling to be open and vulnerable for fear of getting hurt.

In fact, she had been hurt. Her daughter was born when Cassandra was nearly ten years younger, and the father of her child, an even younger man and a drug addict, had drifted away from their lives. Cassandra, it was becoming clear, was a person who could reach for anything, but who did not set very high goals for herself. Her new, irresistible boyfriend turned out to have his own substance abuse problems, and she soon left the relationship, tantalizing though it was.

We talked about the underlying *truth* of her circumstances, that there was a schism between her *desire* and what she *prayed* for and that Cassandra's spiritual challenge centered around grappling with the issue of self-esteem and the recognition that believing in herself was her biggest challenge. She no longer accepted what was less than the best, for herself or for her daughter, and ended this unhealthy relationship. Cassandra is beginning to become consciously aware of how the concepts of *truth, desire,* and *prayer* can combine to form a revelatory whole and guide us toward healthy relationships and more satisfying living.

The *Jupiter mount* is very pronounced on my own hand. I am not surprised by this, because believing in miracles has become second nature to me. But believing in miracles was not always my experience, so I do know how surprised we can be when our prayers are answered. Years ago, I went to an encounter, or group therapy, session and was invited to a subsequent workshop that I really wanted to attend. Unfortunately, the workshop cost one thousand dollars, a sum I simply did not have. As part of the "encounter" we were asked to express ourselves without inhibition and I was advised to ask for exactly what I wanted. I prayed for the confidence to do so and called upon the deepest strength I had. I took a deep breath, stood up in the middle of the discussion, and raised my hand. In ten minutes, that room full of strangers gave me the money I needed, and I was able to continue the workshop. My prayer was answered.

Is prayer really as simple as that? Sometimes we do receive just what we ask for, but more often, it is by engaging in the act of prayer itself that the possibility of *any* result is created. In the case of the encounter group, for example, I prayed for the confidence to ask something of my peers; I did *not* pray for the actual sum I needed. And yet, the result was twofold: my confidence emerged, and so did one thousand dollars.

At the most basic level, prayer is a request or a plea for assistance. Whenever I sit down with a client, the first thing I do is pray for clarity and the ability to speak the truth. I am so aware of the power it has in my life that prayer has become truly sacred to me. Judging from the many pilgrimages people make every year, I am clearly not alone. The ancient Greeks went to the Oracle at Delphi to pray and ask for guidance about the future and to understand the mysteries of the present. The Celtic tribes of northern Europe considered the oak tree (and all wooded areas) to be sacred places where spirits lived and could be contacted. The Wailing Wall in Jerusalem is believed by many Jews to be the holiest place in the world, and hundreds of believers visit it daily. In the United States, Native Americans, who have populated our soil for thousands of years, long-ago identified powerful natural sites that they believed were populated by spirits. Mount Katahdin is one such place, located in Baxter State Park in Maine. The Abenaki Indians believed that this massive granite mountain was guarded by a spirit who presided over the weather. Across the country, the Esalen Hot Springs in California are said to have strong healing powers. There, a creek wends its way to the ocean, surrounded by spring baths.

While these are all well-known examples of sacred places, you may find that your own sacred place is as close by as your favorite armchair. In other words, you do not have to travel to any of these places to reap the benefits of prayer. You need only make the decision to pray. For too many of us, prayer is still not an habitual part of our lives.

Too often, we only turn to prayer when we or someone we love takes ill. To be sure, most sickness is best treated with professional care and medicines, but often illness or pain also exists because of underlying spiritual problems. That is where the idea of *dis-ease* comes into play, and sickness then becomes a metaphor for an underlying reality that we, individually, must learn to recognize. But physical illness is a frightening reality, and it often prompts people to begin to pray. That is because they are scared. I have often seen that when a crisis occurs in peoples' lives, it is then that they become open to new ways of thinking—even to consulting me. I believe, however, that were we to look to God *before* a crisis—that is to say, made prayer a habit—we would be better prepared to deal with it.

Sickness, of course, is not always physical. My troubled home life made adolescence harder for me than it would have been had I been living in a more peaceable home. After my dreadful experience with the social worker in Syracuse and my uplifting palm reading with Florry Nadall, I sought solace and hope in books about palmistry and intuition. I learned that many psychics have near-death experiences, something that was certainly true for me. Mine was after a fight with my mother when I was fourteen, over a peanut butter sandwich she did not want me to eat before dinner.

That particular day, I had brought some friends home and made sandwiches for us to eat while we watched afternoon TV. My mother, exhausted from fighting with my father, burst into the kitchen, shouting that I should not eat between meals. She proceeded to smear peanut butter all over my face and hair. Needless to say, my horrified friends left in a hurry, and I ran upstairs to swallow all the pills I could find.

After my stomach was pumped at the hospital, the doctor told me I had actually come close to dying. At that moment, something shifted inside me and I knew I did not want to die. I knew that as long as I was alive, there was the possibility of change. When the doctor asked me why I had done it, I told him it was because my mother would not let me eat a peanut butter sandwich. He laughed. And so did I.

This experience remains so vivid for me because it taught me two amazing things about life. The first was that though I felt terribly alone, I knew I did not want to die. What was more, I also realized that I could make people laugh. And then I had a miraculous thought: if there was a God, I was not alone after all.

It was my choice. Choose God and live. Or die.

Soon after this experience I moved out of the house, became an au pair in exchange for room and board, and finished high school while I began to study palmistry.

And so I lived. Prayer became my foundation of strength and, I am convinced, the well-spring of my intuitive powers. On my *life* line, an *island* sits. Islands, generally speaking, represent depression. Because the island is connected by a *descending branch* (representing disappointment or misdirected energy) to my Venus mount, its location speaks to me of that near-death experience, and I am reminded of this particularly troubling time in my life whenever I study my own hand. Miraculously, I look upon it with gratitude, for that darkest of moments led me to the brightest awakening of my life—a spiritual one.

Welcoming Prayer

For those of you still troubled by the concept of prayer or how it might fit into your daily life, I would like to offer the insight provided by the spiritual teachings of Nur Ali Elahi, from a book of that title written by his son, Dr. Bahram Elahi, a pediatric surgeon who lectures at the Sorbonne in Paris and at Barnard College in New York. Dr. Elahi writes that communication with God takes place through prayer and that the essential role of prayer is as a means by which we are reminded of and can come closer to God. He notes that the world is a "seedbed for the world beyond" and that if we do not wish to leave our souls empty-handed after our physical body expires, we ought never break off communication with God, since forgetting God is like "falling into a fatal slumber."

His words are lyrical, timely, and full of wisdom. Dr. Elahi also reminds us that there are different *stages* of prayer, the first of which consists of an individual's attempt to "become acquainted" with God by expressing certain wishes and creating a "spiritual confidence." It is this level of connection that prepares us for the following stages.

The next stage *excludes* the fulfillment of personal wishes and focuses instead on accepting the final result of any matter we pray about, no matter what the outcome is. To desire anything other than a result, whatever it consists of, is to take away from our store of "spiritual provisions," which grows as we pray and surrender ourselves to the will of God.

The idea behind these thoughts is to *surrender* to the judgment of God, who knows precisely what we need and, further, knows more than we, mere mortals, ever will. Dr. Elahi suggests that "if we insist on having what we think we want," we are doing ourselves and God a great disservice, for we will be using our "spiritual capital" to try to make changes in the temporal world when, in fact, we cannot do this until we lovingly and humbly connect with the spiritual world.

Finally, Dr. Elahi recommends another prayer, offering the idea that "the best prayer is to ask to remain on God's path and for Him to be content with us: 'O God, I want only You, nothing but You. Help me to do whatever You wish, what You love for me to do.' The prayer of someone truly in love with God is a way of drawing nearer to Him. One loves God for what He is. The Holy Imam Ali prayed like this, 'O my Beloved, I do not adore You out of fear of Your fire, nor because I yearn for Your paradise. I worship and adore You because You are deserving of adoration and praise.'"

For years, clients have asked me *how to pray*. Most experts agree that there is no one right way, but it seems that many prayers are answered when those prayers are exact. Let us imagine, then, that there are three steps to successful prayer. The first step is to use the *present tense*, since, in the spiritual realm, time does not exist. There is no past and future, only the here and now. If you have something particular in mind to pray about, consider it in the present tense. For example, rather than praying, "I will need a new car soon," pray that, "My new car is perfect for me." If there is a negative situation at hand, make it positive, as in, "My baby is alive and healthy," rather than, "My baby may die, please help." I'm sure many of you have heard the phrase, "Be careful what you pray for, you just might get it," and that is because negativity has no place in prayer. Though many of us pray about specific situations because we feel we need or want certain things to change, always remember to *turn the results over to the will of God*. Only then does the profound occur. We must always bear in mind, however, that the will of God often does not match our own, and this fact is what truly challenges our faith.

As you pray, feel free to press your palms together in the classic, universal posture of prayer. Not only will you be following in the footsteps of countless souls who have prayed before you, you will also become aware of where and how your *Jupiter mounts* become connected between your hands.

The second step for successful prayer is to *pay attention*. When someone begins to pray, what commonly happens is that what remains after the prayer is the memory of its intensity or how much yearning went into it and the outcome of the prayer itself is ignored. For example, a client of mine began to pray for a new job. When he received a telephone call inviting him to an interview, he declined. The firm was offering less money than he had hoped for. Instead of realizing that his prayer, in fact, had been answered, he began to complain that he was stuck in a dead-end job, so he stopped praying. Had I been in the same situation, I would have paid close attention to that potential interview: Was it right for me? If not, why had it manifested? Had I prayed for a certain dollar figure to accompany the opportunity? As it turns out, my client had not. I would have reconsidered *precisely* how I had prayed, and I would have begun again. One of the many gifts of prayer is that there are no limitations on how often, when, where, or why we pray!

The third step in the process of prayer is to *respond*. Regardless of whether you have paid attention to the outcome of your prayer or not, or whether you have experienced the desired outcome, you are called upon to exercise humility and *thank God*. The idea behind this thought, according to the learned spiritualist Emmet Fox, is that it is God who does the work of prayer, not us. We are only the channel through which the divine action takes place. Remember that you can turn to God with all your troubles—health, financial, social, sexual, professional—and if you do, I can guarantee that your anxiety will lift immediately. And at that moment, rather than thinking further about your troubles, you should be thanking God instead.

This week, take out your *Desire Map* and begin a new page. Spend some time writing down all the negative aspects of your life, all your fears, shames, and regrets. Make a list of everything that is bothering you. When you are done, literally rip that page from the journal and *burn* it. Then make another list of all the positive changes you would like to make happen (for example, finding a new job, meeting new people, having deeper relationships, experiencing a more satisfying love life, making more money). Whatever your thoughts are, simply write them down. Then, at the bottom of the page, write the word *Amen*. For that word is the stamp of your own acceptance of the possibility of realizing these dreams. Wherever you pray—in synagogue or church, or in your own shower—remember this list. Think of what you want from life, then pray for the willingness and strength to turn those desires over to God.

Until prayer itself becomes a habit, your biggest challenge may be to banish doubt. I hope you will return to this exercise whenever you are doubtful or face new challenges. And that you will continue to create new lists and invite God into your life so you can reach your dreams.

As we have seen, there are so many ways to offer our lives to God's care. Because I live on the shore, I often go to the ocean to pray, surrendering my worries to the sea. When I cannot get to the water, I put my prayers in a *God Can,* something that I made from a simple tin can that is like a bank with a slit on top (you can make your own). I drop my prayers into the slot, literally watching them go out of my hands, and I feel instant relief each time I realize, *When I cannot, God can!*

More than anything else, I pray to remain open and willing. For that is what leads us to true happiness and peace.

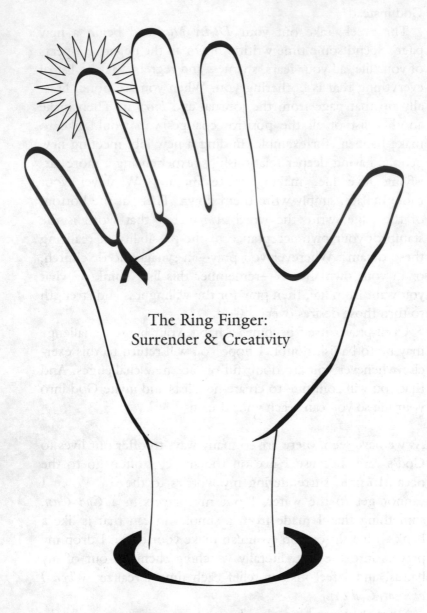

The Ring Finger:
Surrender & Creativity

*The Ring Finger Expresses Our
Creativity, and Indicates Our Need for Surrender.*

TEN

Surrender and Creativity: The Ring Finger

The human hand makes over a thousand different movements every day. Those many movements provide a thousand opportunities to be *seen* and understood. The part of our hand that is the most closely connected to our public personas and relationships is the *ring* finger, the third finger from the thumb. This finger tells the world what we want it to know, for example, that we are married or single.

Our fingers, more than any other part of the hand, express our uniqueness as individuals and reveal more about our true personalities than the lines or markings of our palms (which more significantly represent experiences or potential). In the case of the *ring* finger and its mount, the *Mount of Apollo*, the presence of creativity and an appreciation of the aesthetic qualities of life are revealed.

My client Monique, a young hairdresser whose ring finger literally *itched* when she came to see me, desperately wanted to marry her employer, with whom she was having an affair. However, he was already married. I told her that if she would let this man go, she would then find her true love and would look back at this current relationship as a big mistake. She did not like this reading, especially because her boss had said that he would leave his wife and marry her. I sensed that he was lying and told Monique. Her *large, stiff* hands revealed cautiousness coupled with dedication to hard work. It was also no surprise that she had gravitated toward her current career: large hands paradoxically reveal a detail-oriented nature and hairdressers literally split hairs. Though she did not believe what I told her then, Monique surrendered to her own intuitive process and soon ended the relationship. In six months a wonderful man came into her life, and I have the pictures to prove what a gorgeous wedding they had.

Monique's story reminds me of one I heard about an old donkey that had fallen into an abandoned well. The farmer who owned the animal decided it would be too much trouble to save such an old beast. Instead, he called upon his neighbors to help put the donkey out of its misery, and they all began to shovel dirt onto the poor animal's back. The donkey soon panicked, kicking the well walls with all his might. He twisted and shook to free the dirt from his back, and as he did, a thought came to him: each time a shovelful of dirt fell, he would shake it off and step up. No matter how painful it was, he would shake the dirt off and use it for leverage. Each time the old donkey began to panic and revert to kicking the walls of the well once more, he would remind himself to shake off the dirt and step up. What could have buried him had actually blessed him, and it was not long before the exhausted animal was able to step triumphantly out of the well.

Because of the way the donkey handled that dire situation, he was able to survive. At some point in our lives, each of us is faced with seemingly insurmountable obstacles. There are moments when we think we can only kick the wall, but as the donkey's story illustrates, we have a choice to surrender to our circumstances and find our way out from there. If we first surrender, we will eventually step free of any situation.

Just beneath the *ring* finger is the *Mount of Apollo*, which represents creativity in all forms—our love of music, art, beauty. A *high, firm* Mount of Apollo indicates a love of beauty and a propensity for making an environment warm and cheerful. A *flat* mount reveals a lack of creative energy, which may simply mean that you prefer to observe, rather than participate in, the arts.

If your Apollo mount or ring finger has a *dot* on it, you have probably turned away from artistic pursuits. If a *square* is present, you are a person of great control and level-headedness, artistically or musically inclined. *Grilles* in the area indicate potential artistic talent, but a lack of discipline or motivation toward realizing these gifts. A *star* on the mount reveals a desire to show off and possibly an early or brief success in an artistic career, such as we see with child prodigies who as they age become more average in their skill levels. A well-defined *triangle* indicates true brilliance and talent for its lucky bearer, and a *cross*, conversely, expresses a lack of self-confidence, and thereby limited success in expressing artistic talent.

The ideal *finger of Apollo* is slightly longer than the *index* finger and shorter than the *middle* finger by about the same amount. *Long, straight* ring fingers are often found on the hands of actors or people who work with the public, yet these same people may also possess an introverted nature. An *exceedingly long* Apollo finger most likely belongs to a charmer who others love to be around, but it also suggests that you may be prone to gambling and risk taking that can threaten your relationships.

A *short* ring finger (shorter than the *index* finger), however, indicates that you may need a little prodding to believe in yourself; oftentimes, you may focus a lot of attention on family and friends, rather than on your own artistic aspirations. You are likely to experience frustration as you approach your goals, feeling that you are underappreciated.

An Apollo finger that bends toward the *middle* finger reveals a tendency to rely on professional titles or roles (such as *mother, lawyer*) for your sense of identity and also to overestimate others, which often results in disillusionment and disappointment. A ring finger that bends toward the *pinky* finger may signal a certain dissatisfaction with your environment and possibly a feeling of paralysis before being able to initiate change.

Whether your finger of Apollo is short or long, bent or straight, the information it gives you about yourself is not meant to provide the fuel for self-condemnation. Rather, it provides a starting point by which to identify your own strengths and weaknesses and should serve as an invitation to begin letting go of destructive and limiting preconceptions and guide you to greater self-knowledge.

Tina is a dark, sultry woman in her late thirties. Her *soft, fine* skin and *small, oval-shaped* hands express her emotional, sensitive, and overtly sensual personality in a way that words never could. However, she began our reading by stating that ever since she danced in *The Nutcracker* at the age of three, she has dreamed of becoming a professional dancer. Unfortunately, her battle with her weight began at this same early age. While Tina looked absolutely perfect to me, I know that a dancer's ideal weight is very difficult to maintain. According to Tina, she has always been at least ten pounds too heavy. Judging from the many *islands* covering each major line of her hand, it was obvious to me that Tina had struggled with this issue a great deal over the course of her life, and I sensed that she was terribly hard on herself. That she was, in fact, her own worst enemy. "Good enough is not enough," she later told me. "I have to be the best or nothing."

Constantly second-guessing her talents and unable to surrender control of her destiny, Tina would approach a dance recital with extreme discipline—overpracticing, eating a strict diet—until just a day or two before the performance, when she would overeat and dance all night at clubs and exhaust herself, thereby completely sabotaging her efforts. By the age of twenty five, "Time was running out," she said. "If you're not in a company by then, forget it." As it turned out, Tina was not in a company, and that was when she began to get involved in abusive romantic relationships that mirrored her own self-destructiveness and lack of self-love. She had eventually married a man who belittled her attempts at dance as much as she did.

Tina had long, tapered fingers and a fleshy *Mount of Venus*, indicating true natural passion. Yet, her *Mount of Apollo* was marked with a dot, suggesting that she had possibly turned away from some artistic pursuit. Her *ring* finger was bent toward *Saturn* (the *middle* finger), revealing her overidentification with roles (wife, dancer). Her tendency to overestimate the goodness of others often resulted in her being hurt when the people in her life did not follow through on their promises. "Depending on people who disappoint you will only make you disappointed in yourself," I said. "You are clearly a talented person. Whether you know it or not, you could handle *three* careers." Tina glared at me as I pointed out that her *head* line had a *triple prong* at the end, representing divided abilities, which meant that she truly could manage three avocations simultaneously. "Well, I have a picture-framing business," she finally admitted, "and I am a watercolor artist."

When I prodded her about her dancing career, Tina replied curtly, "My father was right. He said I would never be successful in it." Clearly, she was angry and hurt. "Tina," I said, "your life is not about what your father believes, but about what you do." I told her the truth as I saw it—that she was talented in many areas and that if she considered *teaching* dance, she might be able to heal some of her own wounds. What if she dedicated herself to teaching children to dance without losing themselves, as she had, in the process?

At first, Tina resisted my suggestion. Eventually, however, she started a local dance company and began to work with children. After letting go of her dream to dance professionally, Tina's dream was actually transformed into something larger and she received a grant to teach dance to underprivileged kids in the city. The last time I saw her, she was beaming. Tina had lost those extra ten pounds and had even walked away from her abusive marriage.

Life can be very confusing and painful when we spend all of our energy and talent trying to please other people. For many women, wanting to prove someone wrong or trying to convince others to see us differently, as Tina did with her father, only thwarts our ability to realize our true and God-given potential.

At twenty-eight, Ming Luu was despondent. She had left behind a career in computers because she wanted to become an actress. After some unsuccessful efforts at finding work, she and Jason, her television producer boyfriend, broke up. When Jason fell in love with an actress who appeared on his TV show, Ming Luu was sure she would never find love again. One look at her hand told me otherwise, and I pointed it out to her immediately. Stemming from the *love* line, beneath the pinky finger, were the *horizontal* lines that indicate marriage. "In a year or so, another love will fill your life," I said. "In the meantime, you have plenty to do." But information of this kind does not often heal the wounded spirit of a young woman, and Ming Luu merely shook her head in disbelief. Her *narrow* hands, which can indicate a certain rigidity or stubbornness, foretold this response.

I noticed that her *heart* line was crossed with *chains*, and this indicated a certain instability in the area of love in her life. Her *Mount of Apollo* was covered with a *grille*, revealing that some potential talent was blocked by a lack of discipline or motivation. Ming Luu's *ring* finger was shorter than average, and this meant that she was apt to experience frustration when seeking approval from others and that she probably needed some prodding to believe in herself. I asked Ming Luu then to pray for a moment and look to her higher power when I asked this question: "Why want a man who doesn't want you?" The look in her eyes told me that Ming Luu knew precisely what I meant, but she again shook her head, and uttered meekly, "If I got a job as an actress, then Jason would pay attention to me."

It was my turn to shake my head. I saw that Ming Luu was often motivated by jealousy, which was revealed to me by her excessively long *heart* line, which disappeared at the joint between the *middle* and *index* finger. Her long *thumb* also indicated her willfulness, which could manifest as a stubborn refusal to see the truth of a situation. All of these characteristics and traits were holding her back from her true promise, for Ming Luu was indeed very talented. I told her that I saw her moving to California in the near future and finding work in the computer industry again.

For the first time in our session, Ming Luu's gloomy expression changed. She had left her computer career for Jason, she said, and she used to live in California. "Well, you're going back," I said. But Ming Luu remained stubbornly despondent: "I wanted to belong in the world of entertainment. I thought if I could fit in, Jason would love me more." I told her that she was unique and talented, and that she would be appreciated by others who saw her gifts for what they were. "God has different plans for you. You need to let go of your plans first before his can have a chance."

I told her that if she were meant to be with Jason, she

would be. The *truth* was, Ming Luu had no *desire* to be an actress, but rather than *praying* for a sign from her higher power as to her next move in life, she was stubbornly clinging to a relationship that was alive only in her own imagination. She refused to *surrender* to her true artistic and creative calling, not on stage but in front of a computer terminal.

By the end of our meeting, Ming Luu admitted that her feelings about Jason were bordering on obsessive. "When you let go of your obsessions," I counseled, "you will find your true path." To do so, of course, Ming Luu had to first surrender to her powerlessness over her situation. Was she hurt enough yet to do so? Ming Luu left my house in tears.

Some months later, I received a letter. Ming Luu had moved back to San Jose, California, she wrote, and in less than a week after arriving, she had landed a fabulous job designing and creating educational software. For the first time in a long while, she felt her life was progressing. It was thrilling to hear that Ming Luu had surrendered to one of life's hardest truths: changing yourself in order to make someone love you simply does not work. There is a divine plan for every one of us, and when we surrender to the truths and the mysteries of the universe, the life that we are meant to live, creatively and authentically, becomes ours for the taking.

Sometimes letting go of what we think we want is the only way to ultimately succeed in getting what we really want and need. Releasing our stranglehold on results is one way that creativity, the ultimate expression of the individual self, is born. Early palmistry texts claim the ring finger as the *finger of the Sun*. Apollo was the sun god, and the sun is both the creator and maintainer of life here on earth. Creative energy, then, is inherent in this finger, and because Apollo was capable of both creativity and of destruction, our creative energy can be either positive or destructive. That is why it is crucial that we treat this part of ourselves with honor and respect.

This is also why surrender is such an essential aspect of spiritual growth. Paradoxically, surrendering is not something we can decide to do; it is not something we can control with willpower. Surrender is, instead, something we *experience*. Often, it is accompanied by a package full of difficult feelings—hopelessness, rage, sadness—but it is always followed by release and relief. This is the grace that is at the core of surrender. During the process of surrender, we may likely encounter extremely uncomfortable emotions—frustration and anger at God, at other people, at ourselves—before we fully release our fear and anxiety. In this state of process, it feels impossible to *let go,* but surrender is what is being asked of us at each moment of discomfort; it is at this time that God provides comfort and promises freedom to each of us.

Events in my own life have shown me just how difficult this concept is to grasp. I had my second child at the age of forty-two, and the baby was three weeks late. When labor finally began, it was agonizing. As much as I wanted to experience natural childbirth, I did not want the pain that accompanied it. After twenty hours of labor my doctor offered me the option of taking medication. That is when the nurse held my hand and whispered, "We only get as much pain as we can handle." I squeezed her hand gratefully and began to cry. In that moment, I surrendered. The baby would be born in God's time—not mine. Incredibly, the unbearable pain became bearable, and my son Alex was born, naturally, twelve hours later. For me, being fully conscious while witnessing the miracle of his birth forever deepened my appreciation for the wonder of life and for God's grace at the moment of surrender.

Childbirth, of course, is an extreme situation, and I readily admit that letting go of control in other situations has not always been easy for me. Even if I choose to ignore this stubborn aspect of myself, the wide space between my *head* and *life* lines doesn't allow me to for long; it is a clear and ever-present reminder that I need to work on being less impatient in my life.

When we try to make situations more to our liking by manipulating them, it is less likely that circumstances will change to suit us. Like Monique's, the flesh around my ring finger *itches* when I am preoccupied with controlling other people or situations. I could not force my son Alex's birth any more than I can force a flower to grow. In nature, fish swim and birds fly, enacting their intrinsic natures. Fish do not *try* to swim, nor do birds *try* to fly. The mistake we humans often make is to *try* to make ourselves happy, as if we had the precise formula for how to do this. Since it is impossible to control everything around us, more often than not, we decide what unhappiness is: *If I do not marry by the time I am thirty, I will never get married. If I am not rich by the time I turn forty, I will forget my dreams and work for the city.* Mandates such as these only make us miserable by depriving us of appreciating the gifts and possibilities that currently surround us. They take us out of the present moment and leave us yearning for an always unattainable *then*. It is when we are able to let go of what we think we want that we end up getting what we need and often, much, much more. When we surrender, we are free to enjoy the creativity of the present moment for the rest of our lives.

Learning to surrender, however, is a lesson we must learn again and again. Olivia's story illustrates how difficult this can be. Olivia, a woman of forty-seven, called to make an appointment, and then changed it three more times before finally coming to my office. On the phone, she admitted that she had a hard time surrendering to another person's ideas and this explained why it was so hard for her to commit to our appointment. Yet, she eventually did show up.

Olivia was a short, compact person. Her rather rough

edges were pulled together in a businesslike way, and she wore short cropped hair, which perfectly topped her no-nonsense attitude. Before sitting down and beginning the session, we shook hands. Olivia's hand was *chubby* and *short*, which immediately indicated to me that she was impatient, impulsive, liked good food, and had an erotic imagination. This was clearly an interesting person.

As soon as we sat down, Olivia declared, "I'm here for one reason only, and that's all. I don't want to hear any stuff about past lives and all that mumbo-jumbo." Not unlike a lot of clients, Olivia knew she was unhappy about certain parts of her life and was probably clueless about others. I asked her to slow down and stop talking, so that we might begin the session with some deep breathing. She quickly told me that that's not what she had come for: she had spent her whole life breathing, hadn't she? I told her that it was beneficial to create a safe space between us and that simple breathing would provide this. I also told her that I am not a psychic machine capable of only blurting out the precise information she wanted to hear. She then relaxed and let me begin my work.

"The intuitive process that we are embarking upon," I explained, "is not only going to supply the information that you are consciously seeking. It also provides healing for your spirit. As such, it would be useful for us to develop a little trust between us. Believe it or not, sitting quietly and breathing together really works wonders. Considering that you seem to distrust this process, I will be even more surprised than you if I come up with any information about your past lives."

Somewhat perplexed, Olivia frowned, but at least she was listening to me. "Do you want to proceed with the reading?" I asked. She nodded. "Please give me your hands," I said. And so the reading truly began. Olivia's *thumb* nearly matched the angle of the hitchhiker's, but not quite. This was a sign of her leadership skills, but she also *hid* her thumb, indicating that she had some self-esteem issues present. Her *short ring* finger was *bent* toward the *pinky*, revealing a certain dissatisfaction with something in her environment. Coupling this information with the *descending branches* on her *head* line, my conclusion was that her primary dissatisfaction was with her current career. Lastly, a *small island* at the start of her *life* line indicated a trauma of some kind early in her life.

"Olivia," I began, "you are unhappy with your career because you feel that you are being taken advantage of and because you yourself feel you are not living up to your real gifts. Most of all, it seems, you fear leaving your job—even if you hate it." Olivia's jaw fell open, and she nodded. "I think I know why you don't go all the way with your career," I added.

As the reading progressed, I learned that Olivia worked in the production department of a film company and that she felt she had worked too hard all these years and was too old, at forty-seven, to be running around like a gofer. The position of the island on her life line told me that she had lost someone in her life when she was very young and I told her so. Again her jaw dropped open. "That's right," she whispered. "It was my older brother. I was four, he was seven. He was my mother's pride and joy." I thought Olivia might break down and cry when I said, "Your parents loved him very much. You, however, were a disappointment to your father." She responded, "When my brother died, all hell broke loose. Nobody could do anything to make my parents happy."

It was obvious that when her brother Kenneth died, Olivia's life, to say nothing of her parents', changed forever. Eventually, her parents divorced, and she was sent to live with her mother's sister. Her aunt began to fill her head with negative thoughts, telling her untrue things, such as that Olivia wasn't pretty enough and that she would never amount to anything. "That's when you started thinking that you weren't good enough to be who you were meant to be and why you are now sitting here, at the age of forty-seven, with a broken heart. I am not surprised at your brusque manner. It is there to hide decades of pain."

At that, Olivia did begin to cry. I consoled her by telling her, quite truthfully, that she had the capacity to change, for everyone does. Her life's promise, I said firmly, lay in her own hands, and I explained to her in detail how she could read the truths her hands revealed. She possessed a vital combination of elements, and I assured her that as a result, she would be able to attain her dreams, whatever they were. As it turned out, Olivia wanted to write a book about her brother. I gently suggested that if she had the willingness to trust and surrender to the real gifts in her own life, she would then realize this dream.

"Let me plant the seeds for you now. Just sit here with your feelings for a while. When you're ready, why don't you begin to write the book for Kenneth by talking to him as if he has been with you always, watching over you and your life? Intuitively, that is where I see success for you." Olivia hugged me after our session, which surprised us both. Several months later, she wrote to tell me that she had struggled and struggled, and when she could not fight anymore, she finally surrendered. Somehow, she wrote, everything in her life became easy after that. She cut her work with the film company to half-time, and she began writing the book she had always dreamed of. Regardless of where this creative work led her, she felt certain that her life was now on its proper course. If that's where surrender had led her, she wisely wrote, she only wished she could have let go of her pain and limiting beliefs many years ago.

WEEKLY EXERCISE
Surrendering and Finding Creativity

This week, return to your journal *after* you complete this exercise, which begins with simply tying a red thread around your *ring* finger. The thread will remind you that you are

"following a thread" to a deeper part of yourself as you identify the special characteristics of the ring finger as they apply
to you, based on the information provided earlier in the
chapter. After you have identified those characteristics, ask
yourself a few questions: *What are my creative talents? What
creative pursuits do I enjoy? Why can't I see what the world
holds in store for me creatively?*

Now, *let go* of any answers. The questions you've just
asked yourself are the beginning of this exercise, and their
answers will soon be discovered. The only thing you need to
remember is that the creative process is within each and every
one of us at all times. Most of us work so hard and stay so
busy in our lives that we cannot even see what is in front of
us, but it is always the answer to our longings, the yearning
for our creativity. As you embark on this journey of surrender, I promise that you will find the answers you seek in
places you never dreamed of.

This week, take a walk each day for at least a half-hour. It
doesn't matter where you go or what you think about while
you are walking. Simply notice what is passing through your
mind, *without* judging it; the red thread on your ring finger
will guide you. As you walk, rub your *thumb,* your will center, against the thread surrounding your ring finger. Simply
allow any thoughts to pass through your mind as you ask
yourself those questions posed above, as well as: *Why am I
here on earth? How can I express it creatively?* As you ask these
questions, allow yourself to notice the scenery nearby, the
trees, the sidewalk, the world around you. I promise there
will be a breakthrough before the week is over, and most
likely, you will find answers that surprise you.

Feel free to write down your thoughts and feelings as they
rise within you, but also remember to think of each walk as a
journey through surrender, for it is only by surrendering the
self we have come to know that we are able to find the

deeper fabric of our creative selves and weave new meaning into our lives.

After the week has ended, continue walking each day. If you simply cannot, at the very least use some of that time to record your experience of surrendering the conscious mind to the higher power when it happens. Also, if you are willing to write with your *nondominant* hand at those moments, you will find that a childlike openness brings you closer to surrendering to the creative process each and every time you pick up your pen.

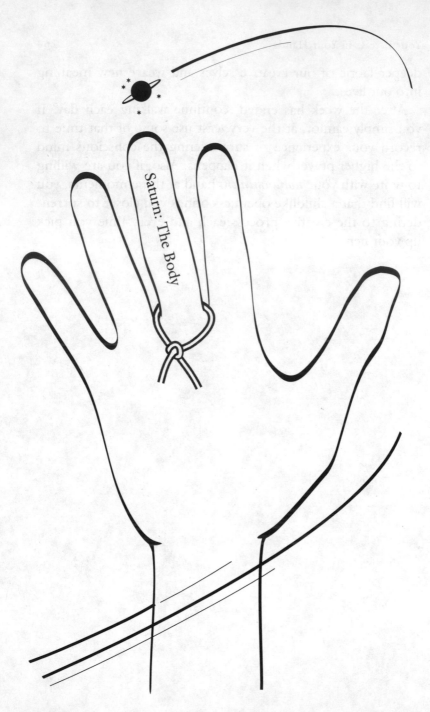

Saturn: The Body

Find Balance for the Body by Reading Your Saturn Finger.

ELEVEN

The Body: The Middle Finger

The *Saturn* (or *middle*) finger is the longest finger on the hand. The *average* middle finger is slightly longer than the *Apollo* (or *ring*) finger, which indicates a balance in both practical and spiritual affairs; if your Saturn finger is *short* (shorter than the ring finger), this indicates a fair degree of impulsiveness, though your impulsive, passionate nature provides energy in creative areas. A *long* finger reveals an analytical, often introspective personality and belongs to those of you who react slowly to outside stimuli, due to your reflective nature.

If your finger is *straight*, a harmonious relationship is likely to exist between mind and body, will and emotion, and social interaction versus isolation; a middle finger that *curves toward the Jupiter* (or *index*) finger reveals a personality that is outgoing and spontaneous. A *curve toward the Apollo* (or *ring*) finger indicates the need to be alone more often than not. *Sharp curves* in either direction indicate imbalances in these areas.

A *knotty* middle finger signals skepticism and a resistance to honoring intuitive impulses; if you have such a finger, you may overly adhere to a system of order in your life. A truly *crooked* middle finger indicates a morbid outlook on life (though this is rarely seen), and a *twisted* middle finger may reveal a tendency to be cruel. The appearance of *vertical lines* on the finger itself suggests an open, frank character, whereas *horizontal lines* indicate a more remote, detached personality.

If your *Mount of Saturn,* located directly beneath your middle finger, is *soft* and *flat,* you are probably very determined and tend to live fearlessly and by your own rules. A failure to look before you leap, however, may result in trouble. A *high, firm* mount indicates the ability to concentrate and a willingness to face challenges if you decide a cause is worthwhile.

As we know, the middle finger is internationally used as a base and ubiquitous sign of displeasure; "giving the finger" or "flipping the bird" is a gesture that grew out of defiance and civil unrest. When the French nobility sought control over English territory during the thirteenth century, they cut off the middle fingers of the rebels, rendering those poor souls useless. Archery was then an essential warfare skill, and without the middle finger native armies could not defend themselves. Following the Battle of Agincourt in 1415, the newly conquered English soon began greeting French court officials with a raised middle finger as a gesture of defiance and vitality.

The truth is, we use our bodies, particularly our hands, to express emotion even when we are not aware of it. When we meet someone, the first thing we usually do is shake hands. In gratitude, relief, or love, we embrace, or pat each other on the back. In anger, we slap or punch. And, in self-hatred, we may even use our own hands to mutilate ourselves.

Just recently, I met with a real estate broker named Allyson. A woman in her early forties, she came to see me because she was experiencing conflicting emotions centering around her marriage of two years. Allyson was both furious and unforgiving of her husband and herself for staying in an unloving, unfulfilling marriage that neither partner seemed able to separate from. Quite unconsciously, she had begun to pull out strands of her auburn hair, twisting it around her Saturn finger. She told me in a hushed voice that the people closest to her, her husband and a coworker, had confronted her with this behavior over dinner one night, and that she had become hysterical.

Allyson's hand was a study in unhappiness. Her *long, thin* fingers topped a *narrow* palm, indicating that she was precise and analytical and apt to be critical in her thinking. Her *heart line* was marked with *chains* in various places, revealing that she had never stopped worrying about or found happiness in her love life. Her *Jupiter* (or *index*) finger *curved* toward her *Saturn* finger, exposing her capacity to be as unsympathetic toward others as she was to herself. Her *Saturn* finger was *sharply* curved toward her *Apollo* (or *ring*) finger, suggesting an inability to balance relationships with the time she needed to spend alone.

I showed Allyson the "facts" that her hand revealed and told her that there was only one way out of her unhappy situation. She needed to acknowledge her own self-destructiveness, which was truly a desperate plea for help. To do this, she would need professional help. Tears filled her eyes and her hands gripped the table as I told Allyson that she needed someone objective in her life to provide perspective and insight about her inability to embrace and enjoy her life.

It is clear that the hand, like other parts of the body, provides information to us about how we feel when our minds may be troubled and unable to discern exactly what the right course of action may be in a certain situation. When we experience a racing feeling in our arms and legs, it may mean, "Danger, get out of here." If we wait too long between meals, our stomach may growl, "Feed me." Too, when we are nervous, our heart speeds up or our hands shake; when we are in love, the sight of our beloved creates warm currents that course through our bodies or cause our erogenous zones to tingle delightedly.

Dr. Deepak Chopra has pointed out that we are a privileged species because we are aware of such sensations. Our nervous systems are aware of the "energy and informational content of that localized field that gives rise to our physical body." And the greater our awareness of this energy "field" the more rich our experience of the world will be.

In my own life, I experience chills when I intuitively flash on an undeniable reality, and this happens often during client readings. I have "trusted my gut" since I experienced that first chill so many years ago, when I "just knew" that my father was coming home unexpectedly. Ancient and medieval thinkers speculated about the precise location of intellectual and spiritual faculties in man, devising theories that separated different areas of the body: the midriff, they believed, was the seat of reason; the gallbladder, the seat of determination; the "guts," the place of courage; and the liver, the seat of emotions. It was believed that the earth's very energy entered through our feet and flowed upward, ultimately reaching our hands. To this day, that energy unwittingly sustains us, whether we are struggling to grow or triumphantly succeeding in doing so.

Too, the "laying on of hands" is a concept that grew from various schools of thought that practiced the art of spiritual healing. In the early 1800s, a Frenchman by the name of Charles Puyan moved to the United States. Touring with a woman by the name of Cynthia Gleason, he proved that while under hypnosis, this gifted woman was able to diagnose illness in others by passing her *hand* over the infirmed's body. Apparently, her diagnoses were accurate enough to create an entire movement, what we have now come to know as "the laying on of hands."

Today, across the United States and most especially in the "Bible Belt" of the Midwest and Southwest this concept has thrived, especially in the Pentecostal movement. There are other groups, in Europe and the United States, such as the White Eagle Lodge in Liss, England, and Lily Dale, in Chautauqua County, New York, where an emphasis is placed on healing through touch.

In Eastern religious groups, it is believed that the vital energy—or *chi*—may be influenced by moving hands over the body. Scientific studies have shown that this form of healing actually increases the oxygen capacity of red blood cells and lowers the high temperatures of those treated. That the belief in the therapeutic benefits of touch has moved beyond religion into the art of physical healing is undeniable.

Life's challenges often appear in the form of physical maladies. When ignored, maladies may turn into disease, and we may find ourselves utterly cut off from our true selves. Some years ago I asked the well-known palmist Nathaniel Altman about the small pearly bumps that I had seen on the thumbs and palms of several clients. He informed me that those translucent yellow or flesh-colored bumps might indicate the presence of cancer. As far back as March 1948, an editorial in the *Journal of the American Medical Association* noted that these particular bumps, or *palmar keratoses,* usually few in number and appearing mainly on the *Mount of Venus* or the *Mount of Luna,* often go undetected.

Since these bumps, however, may indicate the existence of some forms of cancer, they, like *any* lesions, should not be taken lightly. In 1965, Dr. R. L. Dobson and his associates studied 671 patients with proved cancers. They found palmar keratoses in forty-six percent of the men and twenty-six percent of the women. These percentages are significant enough to convince me that, especially in matters of health, the signs of the hand should be taken seriously.

Dr. Theodore J. Barry, another physician working in the 1960s, associated certain particular lines and markings of the hand with no fewer than *fifty* diseases. Today, physicians and other medical professionals are performing ongoing research that links abnormal handprint patterns with dozens of major physical and mental health problems. These include childhood leukemia, schizophrenia, diabetes, congenital heart defects, epilepsy, chromosomal aberrations, thyroid cancer, and Alzheimer's disease.

With this evidence of the hand's capacity to function as a diagnostic aid, we might expect medical palmistry to be more widely practiced. It has been only partially accepted by the medical community, however. Endocrinologists, or gland specialists, for example, have begun to understand that if a person's hand is warm, moist, and tremulous, an overactive thyroid is indicated. In cases of hypothyroidism, or underactive thyroid, the hand is usually cold, dry, and rough.

If we look at arthritis, a common disease of the joints for which there is no known cure, the swelling of the knuckles or joints of the fingers detected early makes effective treatment possible. According to a consensus among arthritis specialists, treatment should begin within six months of the first sign of the disease, before it develops into the crippling and even dangerous condition known as rheumatoid arthritis.

About a year ago, a client named Devorah complained about her husband, Justin. Justin did not believe in doctors, but she convinced him to come see me because he was feeling so bad.

His hands were *broad* and *small* in size, revealing a tolerant personality and an interest in new ideas. His *knotty, sharply curved, middle* finger and the scarred skin of the knuckle clued me in to Justin's poor condition, as did the *descending branches* in each of his major lines, indicating depression or difficulty. But I did not have to be psychic to smell the alcohol on his breath or notice his nicotine-stained fingers. These factors indicated a lack of control. I suspected, based on his strong, independent personality and the deeply etched *head* and *life* lines, that he wanted to own his own business. He agreed. "You can make that happen," I said, "but first you will have to give up your nightly vodka and the three packs of cigarettes a day. You rely on them because you are afraid that you will fail." Justin assumed that Devorah had told me this information, but I assured him she had not. "And," I warned, "if you do not change your habits, you will have a heart attack."

It didn't surprise me that Justin had tears in his eyes at that moment. I had said the words he feared yet needed to hear most. Often people are longing to awaken spiritually, but they do not know how to get there on their own.

The very next day Justin had a heart attack. After three weeks in the hospital he had quit drinking and smoking, had begun therapy, and had started his own business, a marketing company. When I saw him again a year later, the descending branches on his life line had disappeared completely.

Justin's reeking breath and stained fingers had been a tangible form of his unhappiness, but the new gleam in his eye was evidence of a changed man. Once on a spiritual path, your body will tell you what is true and, if you are willing to listen, instinct will replace doubt.

Your body is also capable of healing itself. As Plato wrote, "You don't cure the body with the body, you cure the body with the mind." While the idea of healing ourselves is not at all new, actual proof of this phenomenon is relatively new. Richard C. Moss is a holistic practitioner who developed a series of workshops intended to aid those individuals suffering from catastrophic illness and disease after he himself experienced a spiritual and physical awakening. The true story that follows is a quote from Moss's book, *The Black Butterfly,* and tells of one of his workshop participants.

It was the second day of the conference. For several hours Laura had been singing a childhood hymn, repeating it over and over. Suddenly the quality of her singing changed. She felt as though she were no longer singing. She was the song. She found herself lifted to her feet, her arms raised toward the sky, her head arched upward. She said her hands did not end at her fingertips, but continued into the air and sky. The air and sky were alive, and she and they were the same. Her feet seemed to disappear into the earth. Earth, feet, body, arms, sky, song, singer—all were one living being. Laura did not consider what was happening, it just took her. She was the experience.

The next day her terminal liver cancer was gone. The grapefruit sized bowel metastasis that she had supported with her hand was gone. Three days later she realized that for the first time in thirty-eight years she hadn't taken her daily insulin injections. In the ensuing weeks, all the secondary complications of her diabetes and cancer—kidney failure, fluid in her lungs, tumor-ridden lymph nodes, partial blindness, loss of sensation in her hands and feet, addiction to pain medication—healed. Even a few recently broken toes were completely mended within days. She was radiant; a palpable presence poured from her body like a gentle flame and the whole understanding of her life was radically transformed.

This incredible story proves the power the human mind has over the body. As the new millennium begins, I am pleased to report that medical science has begun to accept what many of us who travel on different paths have long known: attitude is everything.

Ignoring our own intuition, whatever it may be, can cause harm. I have learned this the hard way in my own life. Each week, I meet with a group of women who are either writers or artists. The goal of our meeting is to support each other so that we may each accomplish our artistic goals. To this end, we list the activities that we wish to accomplish that week; for example, Jody wants to finish writing her grant proposal, Jean-Marie wants to complete a painting, Elaine wants to compose an artist's statement. I spend a substantial amount of time developing my workshops in the group and, of course, writing this book. In addition to the many projects I hope to accomplish each week, I always mention getting fit as one of my goals.

Part of how the group operates is that we follow up on a person's list of goals from week to week, using a simple *did-you-do-what-you-said-you-would-do?* approach. And most of us do most of what we say we will, though sometimes, of course, half of us do everything and the other half, nothing, since life events and situations do influence how much of this wish list we can accomplish. Each week, I talk about my desire to lose weight, exercise more, and improve my general level of fitness. After hearing me talk about this issue without really getting anywhere for a full year, one of the bolder women in the group said, "Maybe you should try OA—Overeaters Anonymous." My face flushed deep red, and I immediately blurted out, "No way! I am *not* going there!" My group lovingly pointed out how defensive I became at this simple suggestion. Perhaps it was because of how loudly I had shouted, "*No way*"—I bet it could be heard all the way in the kitchen of the restaurant—but my group reminded me that the path of most resistance is often the best path to take. They suggested that I at least consider putting an OA meeting on my list. Grudgingly, I agreed.

A few days later, in the midst of a particularly stressful week, I sat typing at my computer with a box of chocolate chip cookies right beside me. When a chocolate chip became wedged between the *j* and *k* of my keyboard, I began to admit that I might indeed have a problem, but not until some crumbs became wedged between the *z*, the *x*, and the *c*, did I accept that I really *did* have a problem. Taking care of the household, my boys, and their father, writing a book, producing a television show, and developing new workshops all at once had begun to take its toll on my stress level and my waistline.

I thought of my group and how they suggested that I just try an OA meeting once. That's when I turned off the computer and made a phone call to a person I knew who attended these meetings. On the following Saturday morning, I found myself pulling up in front of the local senior citizens center bright and early. Taking a deep breath, I walked into the room fifteen minutes before the meeting was scheduled to begin. Inside, there were about a half dozen men and three or four women. At first glance, they were average looking—some slim, some on the heavy side—and most looked as if they might need to lose only about ten pounds; I was amazed that there weren't more significantly overweight people in the room.

I closed the door behind me, feeling comfortable enough to say, "I'm so glad I got here. I haven't been able to stop doing it all week. Everything in the house has been going directly into my mouth!" The group looked at me a bit strangely. Finally, one of the older men said softly, "This is an SLA meeting. You sure you're in the right place?" "What's

SLA?" I asked. "Sex and Love Addicts Anonymous," he replied.

I felt my cheeks flush with embarrassment. When I am embarrassed, I often try to disguise my discomfort with humor, so I continued, "Well, if I were having more sex, maybe I wouldn't be eating so much!" Some of the people laughed, but the gentleman who had pointed out my error looked at me with a very serious expression on his face. "You know, you might belong here anyway," he said, handing me a pamphlet. The front page of the pamphlet read, *Questions to ask yourself if you are a Sexual Anorexic.*

The very idea that *I,* with my extra pounds, could be anorexic made me laugh out loud. After thanking him, I found my way to the next room, where the OA meeting was usually held, but this week, it had been canceled. I plan to try again, but in the meantime, I've started walking every day and I've incorporated meditation into my walk. I've lost a few pounds, too, but more than anything, I'm finally experiencing the peace of mind that comes from listening to what your body needs.

If I am willing to look at my hand to discover different aspects of myself, I know that I can look at the rest of me too. I've certainly lived long enough to realize that what we resist persists in our lives and that becoming willing to face my core issues can be as life changing as surgery. By the time this book is published, I will have lost or gained weight. Because the truth is, like all the other aspects of my life, my weight is in my own hands.

When we refuse to listen to our bodies or our minds, we often find ourselves enveloped by fear. Lionel is a sales vice president and thirty-eight years old. He travels a great deal and sees his wife and three small children only on weekends.

Clearly concentrating on his responsibilities to his job and family, Lionel puts himself last, a reality made obvious by the extra sixty pounds he was lugging around when we met at a Citibank party in New York City not long ago. Several of the men at the party at first did not admit that they wanted readings, and many joked about my being a gypsy fortune-teller who had come to predict doom and death. Death is precisely what many men fear, and it is often impossible for them to discuss death and illness frankly, especially with an intuitive. My standard reply to their good-natured ribbing is that I will not talk about death and dying unless I am paid in advance. This response usually elicits a big laugh, helping to soften their resistance. That night, a few bankers sat with me for short readings before heading over to Lionel's table. "She was right on with me," they both said. And so Lionel's curiosity finally got the best of him, and he ambled over to my table and sat down.

What I first noticed on his palm was a bright red *dot*, indicating a shock of some kind. Because of its location on his *head* line, I knew the dot had something to do with his work life. His *Saturn* (or *middle*) finger was very *long*, suggesting an analytical nature and probable resistance to making changes; this was combined with a *knotty* knuckle, which told me I sat before a very skeptical man. The overall *soft* texture of his hand revealed a sensitive nature and his *well-developed Venus Mount*, marked by a *horizontal lines*, indicated a passionate, yet troubled nature. All told, Lionel's anxious demeanor was not at odds with his palm.

I closed my eyes and saw him holding a young woman. "I feel you have had a great shock at work," I began. "You experienced the death of a coworker recently." Tears welled up in me, and as I opened my eyes, I saw that Lionel was also crying. He nodded and told me that just two weeks earlier, Charlotte, his twenty-nine-year-old secretary, had suffered an aneurism, fallen into his arms, and died. For the past two weeks, all he could think about was death. When he thought of Charlotte, Lionel could not stop imagining himself dying. What would become of his wife and kids? Who would take care of them?

I listened to Lionel, who was indeed suffering. While I did not want to upset him further, I did want to show him that he had been presented with an opportunity to make some needed changes in his own life. I gently ran my finger along the base of his middle finger, his *Mount of Saturn,* and noticed a small *wart.* "Lionel," I said, "there's a reason you have this wart on this finger, and it's not because you like to play with toads." He laughed. "The wart shows me that you are busy taking care of others, but not yourself," I continued. "I know we all take our health for granted, but this little bump is your body's way of telling you to pay attention to it, treat it in a more healthy manner. The simple fact is, without a healthy body you won't be able to take care of anyone else at all."

Lionel sat shaking his head. Like many men, he did not want to take responsibility for his own health, he just wanted to assume he was healthy. Yet his own body was giving him an undeniable message. It took a few years, and the discovery of a polyp in his colon, before Lionel finally changed his diet and made exercise a part of his life.

Western medicine tends to treat the body like a machine. When an illness arises, its symptoms, rather than its cause, are usually treated. In my own life, I have struggled with my weight since childhood. Rather than looking at the cause of my struggle, I have chosen the "quick fix" again and again. During my twenties, when I was most obsessed with the extra twenty pounds I carried because of my acting career, I went so far as to allow a dentist I was dating to wire my jaw shut. He went on vacation, and I gained ten pounds, managing to slurp down more milk shakes than ever before through the straw that enabled me to eat. Though a closed mouth stopped me from saying a few things that were probably better left unsaid to the dentist when he returned from vacation, it certainly did not change my appetite or that empty feeling in my gut that called out to me, as if it had a mind of its own, constantly.

The fact is, neurobiologists have recently discovered that we possess not one but two brains, one encased by our skulls and one in our gut. The "second brain" is known as the enteric nervous system and is located in the lining of the esophagus, stomach, small intestine, and colon. Research has shown that the cells in these tissues are the same cells found in the cranium and form a network of neurons, neurotransmitters, and proteins that support a complex circuitry, making it possible for us to learn, remember, and experience "gut feelings."

Letitia is an architect in her late forties who had never had a reading with a palmist or psychic before she came to see me. Her hands were *small* and *firm*. Small hands, indicative of a sensitive and lively nature, fit so well on someone who likes to see the big picture, as an architect must. The firmness of her hands revealed an energetic, active individual. At the area indicating the present on both her *heart* and *life* lines, *islands* existed, indicating depression or emotional trouble. And her life line was actually *broken,* revealing that she had experienced a sudden shock. I noticed, too, the *double line* of her life line, which let me know that she had her own guardian angel and that this being was helping her through difficult moments even as we sat together. Though it was a hot summer day, chills began to travel up my right side as I said, "You have lost someone you love." Letitia immediately began to weep. "It was your husband," I continued, "and he died long before his time—a sudden death that was painful but fast."

As if it were a dream, the whole scene opened up to me and I saw the two of them in France. Her husband had been misdiagnosed and suffered a brain virus that brought him to a Paris hospital emergency room on a weekend holiday. He died two hours later. Letitia had come to see me because she was simply sick with grief, unable to absorb the shock of her husband's death and the responsibility of caring for her three-year-old son. She had stopped eating days before and was rapidly becoming weak.

Rather than concentrating on death, I pay attention to life and its possibilities, and so I did not withhold another picture that came to me: Letitia would marry again, becoming involved with a loving man who would not only father her son but love her unconditionally. I sensed that the husband she had lost really wanted her to go on with her life, even though his life had ended so abruptly. Letitia sat hunched, her arms wrapped around her gut as I told her this. But she gradually straightened up and stopped clutching at her grief. That was the moment I saw drums and, in a flash, recognized the red hair on her husband Jerome's head.

At that moment, I realized I had known Jerome too. Twenty years earlier, we had both been single and had dated for a time. As the chills overtook my body I grew uncertain. Should I tell Letitia this? Momentarily stunned, I felt telling her was the most truthful thing I could do, and yet, I hesitated.

Letitia composed herself and left quickly, promising that she would soon return for another reading with her son. When she did, I began to explain what had happened during our last session, but Letitia interrupted me. She had told her lawyer about our previous meeting, and as life itself can seemingly turn the world into a small place, her lawyer, also an old friend of Jerome's, knew who I was. Gazing at the face of Jerome in her boy's face, we embraced, expressing our belief that Jerome himself had sent her to see me so that she might experience closure to the relationship and move ahead.

As fate would have it, Letitia eventually married her lawyer, yet another gift from her husband, I like to believe. Whenever I think of this story, I look up into the heavens and smile at Jerome, delighted by the special care he provided for his family.

I knew Jerome at a time when I was extremely uncomfortable about my own body. Looking back at my early life, it is no surprise that my journey through puberty and into adulthood was fraught with feelings of shame and humiliation. Outside appearances meant everything to my parents, and though I did not put on extra weight until my later teens, everyone in my family was self-conscious about physical appearances. My parents were slim and quite attractive, but each of them worked at being so: when my father gained a few pounds, he stopped drinking beer and replaced it with Rhine wine and no dinner; my mother took "pep" pills, a common practice among women in those days, and so she was high-strung and nervous most of the time.

Though the idea of "shame" was not common then, the feelings certainly were. At ten years old, my breasts had begun to bud, and I was embarrassed by them. One hot summer day, my father told me to go and play outside with the boys under the sprinkler, who all were shirtless. "I can't go out there," I said. "Sure you can," he insisted, "go on and take your shirt off." I shook my head miserably. My father demanded that I tell him what was wrong.

When I did, he roared with laughter, grabbed some Band-Aids and stuck them on my chest, then shoved me out the door. I felt the heat of the driveway tar beneath my feet and the heat of embarrassment on my face. In time, I learned to face the world with a few extra pounds on me, hoping that men would and would not notice me. Yet as I put on more weight, my desire to be beautiful in the eyes of the world grew accordingly. My lifelong struggle to balance these aspects has brought me to a keen awareness of the damaging emphasis our culture has placed on the "perfect" body.

WEEKLY EXERCISE

Minding the Body

I like to think that perfection is a state of mind, especially in relation to the body. Our five senses, however, enable us to experience life in all its perfection. We see the perfect sunset, hear the perfect symphony, smell the perfect perfume, taste the perfect meal, and touch the perfect hand of someone we love. It is therefore our responsibility to care for our bodies as best we can so that our senses continue to enrich our lives. More often than not, I have found that people choose to focus on the parts of themselves, both mental and physical, that they do not like, rather than celebrating the miracle of life itself. This week's goal is to reconsider our relationship to our bodies.

Does it surprise you to entertain the idea of having a relationship with your body? For many people, the answer is yes. If we focus that relationship on each of our fingers and what their specific information conveys to us, we will begin to see our bodies more truthfully. While we have been pressured by society to become healthy and beautiful on the outside, we have paradoxically ignored our inner health. Return to your journal and write the answer to the following question: *Do you love your body?* Whether your answer is positive or negative, explain why. Not surprisingly, perhaps, more people say no than yes, and then wonder why they feel so bad about themselves. We have all heard that a "man's home is his castle," and while that may be so, it seems just as true that a man's castle is his body, and it should be treated as such, with care and respect.

Many people ignore this simple concept, replacing it with thoughts of being too much of something: too fat, too thin, too old, too young. In reality, we are unique individuals and the only thing there is too much of in this world is negative thoughts. It is now time to transform our negative self-images into positive ones. Begin now by regarding your *middle* finger. What promise does it hold? Review the material earlier in the chapter and make a list of the positive characteristics your middle finger possesses. Next, write down what you interpret as its negative characteristics. For example, you might write: *My middle finger is knotty and curves toward my index finger. This shows that I am outgoing but skeptical.* Is "outgoing" a positive characteristic? Is "skeptical" a negative one? The answers are up to you. As you hold this list in your hand, realize that you can change your perception at any moment. Remember that your thoughts are as powerful as a surgeon's scalpel and perhaps even more dangerous, for only we are capable of leaving scars within our own hearts.

Remember, too, that your thoughts are as powerful as art—painting, sculpture, poetry, music. When Roberta Flack sang, "Strumming my heart with your finger," she was referring to the finger of Saturn, for that is the primary finger used when playing a string instrument—a guitar, cello, harp, or violin. Would that we all thought of ourselves as Stradivarius violins, those precious, priceless instruments. Not only would the world be much more melodious, but so too would we recognize that we are all precious, priceless human beings.

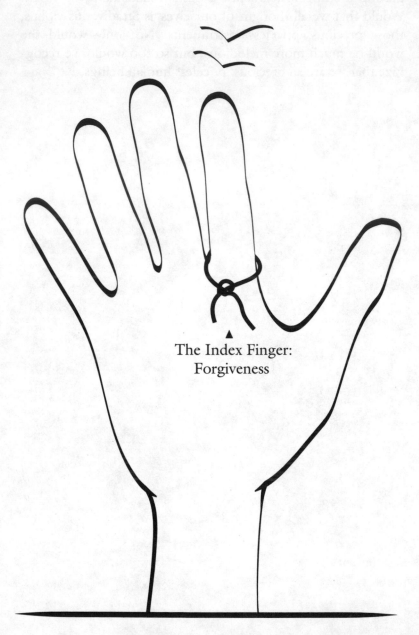

The Index Finger:
Forgiveness

The Index Finger Points the Way to Forgiveness.

TWELVE

Forgiveness: The Index Finger

Because we use the *Jupiter* (or *index*) finger to point to things outside of ourselves, this finger more than any other reveals our relationship to the world around us. We point in an attempt to explain what direction to take or sometimes to draw attention to an object; we press this finger against our lips to ask for quiet or hold it high in the air to indicate caution or warning. We often wag the index finger in admonition, as if it were a small club. In anger, we shake the Jupiter finger threateningly.

Think of the poster of Uncle Sam pointing directly at us with his stiff forefinger below the words, "I Want You," as a recruitment poster for the armed forces. Or think of the unforgettable demonstration of using the index finger in an intentionally intimidating way when President Clinton chose to point his Jupiter finger directly at the television cameras while stating that he had not had an inappropriate relationship with Monica Lewinsky. This was a shockingly aggressive gesture of defiance, especially coming from our commander-in-chief.

185

In my workshops, I often focus on the Jupiter finger. Smokers hold cigarettes between index and middle finger, drinkers grip cocktail glasses between thumb and index finger, and any one of us will often lay our spoon or fork against our forefinger between bites of food. I've used these examples purposefully, for the index finger also represents our tendency toward indulgence. When we overindulge in one area or another, as many of us are likely to do at some point in our lives, we often respond to the indulgence by *blaming* others for it.

Astrologically, Jupiter embodies a tendency toward excess and also toward arrogance. That would explain the tendency to point our fingers at someone in an attempt to shift the *blame* for our transgressions to a real or perceived offender outside of ourselves (think of Clinton wagging his finger at the nation and addressing us all with guilty condescension). We often find ourselves blaming first and then, finding ourselves in the often uncomfortable position of needing to *forgive*—others, perhaps, but often, ourselves. If we do *not* forgive in these instances, we are often nagged by repeating patterns or, worse yet, a distortion of reality, inviting addiction into our lives. No matter how else we may view it, forgiveness is indeed a challenge. And it is only when we forgive ourselves and others for real or imagined injustices that we are able to grow and our level of consciousness may rise or expand to a higher level.

Jupiter also embodies the potential for the expansion of energy, a promise that resides inside each of us, whether we know it or not. In my estimation, an expansion of human consciousness often results when we persevere through hardship, setbacks, and challenges, rather than giving in to the easier action of laying blame.

Because it is obviously such a powerful and vital finger, an analysis of the shape and length of the Jupiter finger enables us to understand our basic attitudes toward life.

The ideal *finger of Jupiter* is slightly *shorter* than the *ring* finger and about half a tip *shorter* than the *middle* finger. A *long* index finger indicates a self-confident attitude that has most likely been yours since childhood, and this is often combined with leadership ability. If the Jupiter finger is *longer* than the *ring* finger, your desire for affluence, pleasure, and comfort may weigh heavily on your daily life, and you may feel as if you are always trying to keep up with the Joneses and get ahead. A Jupiter finger that is *longer* than the *middle* finger indicates a lack of sympathy toward others, since you may be too intent on achieving success. A person with this type of index finger may be aggressive or even arrogant.

Conversely, a *short* index finger may reveal a lack of self-confidence and, if *extremely short,* a sense of inferiority. For those of you with short Jupiter fingers, you are probably more comfortable behind the scenes than directly on stage. Combine this type of index finger with a *short thumb* and you may experience more frustration than others when trying out new endeavors.

If your Jupiter finger is excessively *curved* (almost like a banana), you likely have a great need for security and are prone to take action based on precaution rather than abandon; you may even have a tendency to stock up on supplies or hoard possessions in an effort to feel safe. A *long* and *slightly* curved Jupiter finger can reveal a tendency toward vanity, controlling behavior, or self-centeredness; if this finger curves toward the *middle* finger, you may be not only possessive but jealous.

Thin Jupiter fingers are found on the hands of introverted individuals who may possess a strong aesthetic sense. Similarly, *tapered* index fingers are often found on the hands of artistic or impulsive types. A *knotty* index finger indicates an analytical nature, and bearers of this type of index finger often lack spontaneity and have difficulty expressing their true feelings to others. A *fleshy* index finger points to a hedonistic or narcissistic nature, and people with these personality types often have trouble bonding with others. Finally, a *pointed* index fingertip indicates that religious or inspirational issues may well be a prominent focus in your life.

Warts, cuts, scars, or *dots* on your Jupiter finger indicate some anxiety or worry about abundance in life and correspond to issues we face on a daily basis, such as matters of money, sex, or food. Watch for these superficial markings closely, and you will be better able to pinpoint the sources of worry and anxiety that color your day-to-day quality of life.

In ancient times, the planet Jupiter was believed to symbolize wisdom, generosity, and optimism. But the index finger is sometimes called the *finger of Napoleon,* since it is the finger of ambition. Napoleon's invasion of Normandy certainly expressed his own ambition, but the fact that his Jupiter finger was extremely *short* also revealed his deep-seated insecurity. While ambition and pride are traits surely needed to advance in the everyday world, the index finger also symbolizes vast and untapped wisdom. Because of this, the Jupiter finger offers us the opportunity to reach beyond our limitations and grasp the concept of a higher order. If we are willing to do this, we may expand the breadth of our souls.

But this expansion is not easy. While many of us have heard this line from the poem "An Essay on Criticism," by Alexander Pope, "To err is human, to forgive divine," it may take our entire lives to truly understand its meaning. The need for forgiveness is often brought on by struggling with a great challenge. In my own life, I often face what seem like near impossible challenges in raising my two sons.

One hot summer day several years ago, Alex, my youngest son, sought revenge on his older brother, Danny, who had just called him a "turd boy." Five years old at the time, Alex had a big interest in playing fireman, and after his brother called him that horrible name, he ran outside and grabbed the garden hose. As Danny sat at his computer in their bedroom, Alex sprayed the hose full force on his brother through the window, soaking not only his brother but his computer, their new bunk beds, and the wood floor. When I heard the commotion from the kitchen and ran outside, Alex saw me coming and promptly turned the hose on me. Slipping, falling, and hollering at the top of my lungs, I swore that I would wring his neck with that hose. At that moment, I was clearly a far cry from being a psychic healer or even a loving mother. At that moment, I suddenly remembered a day that I had locked my own mother in her upstairs bedroom when I was about Alex's age. She had eventually climbed onto the roof in her nightgown to call a neighbor for help. It had been great fun for me to lock the door, but I grew terrified at the sound of her angry voice, and as an adult I was able to recall how the idea of her wrath brought forth a paralyzing fear and an overwhelming desire to escape. The serendipitous visit of this memory helped me begin to forgive my son instead of dousing him with that hose, but I was able to fully forgive him only *after* he joined in to clean up the bedroom.

For most of us, it is easy to blame others for our "errs." I blamed my mother for allowing my father to hurt me just as Alex blamed Danny for hurting him by calling him a bad name. Challenging circumstances such as these, however, have led me to understand that when we are open enough to truly forgive, our hearts and minds will only expand.

Frank, an engineer in his fifties, was extremely distraught over the fact that his wife had left him for their next-door neighbor. Though a year had passed since she had left, he was still furious with his estranged wife, and he walked into our session with an "I-want-to-get-even" mind-set. I took Frank's hand and could immediately feel its inflexibility. His *Jupiter* finger was *long* and it *curved* toward the *middle* finger, indicating his possessive and controlling nature. My immediate thought was to tell Frank that he had to forgive his wife and get on with his own life, but Frank only shook his head. "Why did she run off with the neighbor? I was a good husband. I did not deserve this!" I allowed Frank to let off some steam, and I soon sensed why he had really come to see me.

Frank hoped that I would act as a psychic busybody and inform him about his wife's new life. He blurted out his various plans to hide his cash in order to prevent his ex-wife from receiving any alimony, and he wanted me to tell him which one of these plans would be successful. I am always amazed at how fear and a lack of control can cause a person's behavior to change from benign to predatory. I allowed him to release the negative energy he had walked into the room with, and then I studied his hand.

The inflexibility of Frank's *Venus Mount* and, indeed, his entire hand revealed a person with much frustration in his love life, and he was clearly unable to move beyond this state. Not surprisingly, his *heart* line was covered with *islands* and *chains,* which indicated the long-standing nature of his troubled relationship with matters of the heart. I calmly told Frank that I did not invade the psychic space of others, but I felt certain that, despite his enormous pain, he had a chance to move on and grow. Sadly, Frank continued to see me every three months for the next year but always with the same questions about how he could wreak havoc on his wife. But as those months passed, I watched Frank's hand develop a new *marriage line,* and I told him he would get married again. I warned him, however, against jumping into another commitment until he was free of the troubled, malevolent feelings he felt for his ex-wife.

Six months later, Frank did marry again, but the marriage lasted less than a year. Rebecca, his new wife, was more financially solvent than Frank, and before they were married, she bought him a new car. As a wedding gift, Rebecca bought a new house for them; apparently, she loved Frank very much. But Rebecca eventually left Frank, accusing him of having a mistress. The "mistress" in this case was Frank's ex-wife, with whom he was still obsessed. The first thing Frank did when Rebecca ended their relationship was to make an appointment with me. He was more distraught than I had ever seen him, and we sat and prayed together—a first for Frank. Later, I asked him if he realized what had poisoned his relationship with Rebecca, and he nodded slowly. "My ex-wife," he said, "who deserted me." Clearly, this man had a long way to go before he really understood what forces were at work in his life.

Frank continued to consult with me, and he added prayer to his daily life. Gradually he became able to forgive his first wife, and ironically, he is now dating a divorce lawyer and is very happy.

Frank is not unlike a lot of people who find it nearly impossible to forgive someone who has hurt them terribly. Yet, though it took years in Frank's case, he was finally able to forgive and move on with his life. There are many instances, however, when people are *never* able to forgive, and pain, rather than pleasure, takes up permanent residence in their hearts.

To the ancient Romans, Jupiter was the god of the sky, which is limitless. The Jupiter finger reveals to us that we can be limitless too. But because we are so often bound by our ego, which tends to focus on injustice and which is drawn to reactionary behavior (think *"an eye for an eye"*), our ego makes it nearly impossible for us to forgive. What the ego does not know, however, is that in the act of forgiveness, not only may we be surprised to see a situation change radically, we may suddenly find ourselves experiencing unimagined freedom.

Janalea, a friend of another client whom I had never met, called one day in a panic. She could not wait the two days it would take to see me in Manhattan, and so she chose to travel out to East Hampton on the first bus available. An agent for playwrights, Janalea was a tall, professional-looking woman in her late forties. As soon as I saw her at the bus stop, I knew why she had come to see me: she had lost something precious to her, and I said so to her. "How did you know that?" she demanded. She was preoccupied as I drove us to my office, clearly worried over the idea that I could read minds.

When we sat down and began the reading, I examined Janalea's hand closely. Her *small* hands let me know that she wanted more out of life and their *softness* indicated that she was an emotional person. Her long artistic fingers indicated sensitivity and her *pale heart* line suggested that Janalea was prone toward sentimentality rather than true feeling. She had several *descending branches* on her hand, which revealed disappointment in love. Her *long Jupiter* finger expressed her confidence, though its excessively *curved* nature indicated a great need for security. A *wart* sat on the tip of her *index* finger, a clear sign to the world that she was extremely worried about something.

I closed my eyes and concentrated on Janalea's presence, waiting for my sixth sense to focus. Immediately, an image of a broach filled with small but perfect gems, diamonds and rubies, appeared behind my eyes. It was a very old piece, and I immediately described it to Janalea, who gasped with astonishment, since I had described exactly what was missing. She then told me the history of the piece. The broach had come from the estate of a Russian czar and had belonged to her mother's family for more than seventy years. Because both of her parents were dead, the piece was invaluable both financially and emotionally. Janalea was simply desperate to find it, and that is why she had had to rush out to see me. Could I tell her where it was?

I closed my eyes once more and saw the image of a man in his early thirties; a handsome, well-bred person who was most likely British. Janalea turned pale and admitted that her husband fit my description, a man she was presently separated from. "He took it," I said, "because you have not supported him in his career struggle. He's an aspiring playwright, right?" Janalea confirmed this with an angry nod of her head. I advised her to confront him on the matter, certain that the broach would resurface. Janalea remained angry, demanding to know how I knew all this information. "Do you know my husband?" she questioned, unable to believe that I had received this information psychically. Nothing I said would satisfy her.

Janalea returned to the city, but she did not confront her husband directly. Instead, she hired a private detective who ultimately found the broach, which had mysteriously resurfaced in her own apartment; her husband had sneaked in and returned it. Though I had been correct about the nature of her loss, Janalea refused to believe it. In fact, she called me on several occasions insinuating that I had conspired with her husband from the very start. Poor Janalea, she had been so badly hurt by her husband's theft and betrayal that she was unable to forgive him and had transferred her guilt to me.

Though it is the case that forgiving others is almost always a difficult feat, forgiving *ourselves* is often even harder.

Susan was the thirty-something mother of two small children whom I had met at a private party in the Hamptons. The first thing she mentioned when she sat down for a reading was that she was a born-again Christian who really did not believe in "all this psychic stuff." I merely smiled, sensing just how much she wanted to prove me a "fake." When she offered her hand, I glanced at her *children* and *marriage* lines first. "You have three children?" I asked. "Oh, no. I have two boys, ages two and three," she said triumphantly. The markings on her hand indicated that her first child would have been born nearly twenty years earlier, so the idea that her boys were so young did not make sense. Also, the *island* on her *life* line indicated emotional trouble. Her *soft*, somewhat delicate skin had already let me know that she was an emotional individual, most likely sensitive to what others thought of her, so I approached her gently with my next question. "You had a miscarriage early on?" I asked. "I see that you were depressed in your late teens." Instead of answering the question, Susan went pale and tears formed in her eyes. "I don't want to do this," she announced, and left my table.

Before the party ended that night, Susan approached me once more and asked to make a private appointment. Several weeks later, she arrived at my office, and in that short period of time, her hand had changed. Now a *dot* appeared on her *Jupiter* finger, something I had never before seen. "You have had a shock recently," I said. "I sense it has something to do with the night we met." Susan nodded slowly. "I had a baby when I was just fifteen, and I gave it up for adoption. Nobody except my parents knows," she blurted. "I feel ashamed for getting pregnant since my father is a minister—and so is my husband. He has no idea that I had another child before we were married. He thinks I was a virgin when we married." I now understood the meaning of the dot on her Jupiter finger: Susan was harshly judging herself.

It became obvious that Susan did not know how to forgive herself for decisions she had made in her past; she had even begun drinking at night to drown away the memory. A rash had broken out across her torso, which her doctor ascribed to "nerves," and she was not sleeping well. "You are a religious person, Susan," I said softly. "Surely God forgives you, so why can't you forgive yourself?" I suggested that she seek out a therapist or another minister to whom she might process her grief and self-blame. Tearfully she thanked me and left our meeting. A few months later she called to say that she had finally told her husband, who forgave her, but that she was still struggling with forgiving herself.

When I look at my own *Jupiter* finger, I notice how *fleshy* it is, which indicates my hedonistic bent. I admit it, I love sweets! Also, it has a *pointed* tip, which perfectly expresses my spiritual nature. Neither of these characteristics, however, has made it any easier to forgive the people in my life I spent many years blaming for my emotional pain—my parents.

By the time my younger brother, Dennis, was to be married almost twenty years ago, my parents had divorced. I had not seen my father for several years before that time, but as the wedding approached, we all decided, myself and my six siblings, to attend the wedding regardless of the fact that *both* of my parents had agreed to go. My father, however, did not arrive until the day *after* the wedding, when Dennis and his new bride were already on their way to Hawaii for their honeymoon. The job of retrieving Dad from the airport fell to me.

Though I had been through years of therapy by that time, my old anger and pain toward my father resurfaced as I drove to the airport. I had never told him how he had made me feel in my early life and that I could not forgive his behavior toward me. Instead, I continued to avoid those feelings by eating sweets, basically eating my own anger. On the drive, however, I made the decision to talk to him about how much his behavior had hurt, not only me, but everyone in our family.

My father, except for his tired eyes and white hair, looked the same. He sat quietly and listened as I reminded him of all those instances in which he belittled and humiliated me and how his drinking had frightened and embarrassed all of us. I told him how awful it felt not to have had a father to rely on for love or guidance. After I finished, I felt a huge weight of anger and sadness lift, and at that moment, I was able to forgive him. It came as a complete surprise, something like an unexpected bonus, to hear my father quietly say that he was sorry.

When we pulled into my brother's driveway, one of my sisters was waiting for us. The first thing my father did when he left the car was point to me and say, "She's still crazy!" Momentarily, my heart sank, but then it buoyed up, for at that moment, it became clear that it did not matter anymore what *he* thought, it mattered what *I* thought, and I had already forgiven him.

More recently, I was able to forgive my mother for her lack of protection. Only after experiencing life as a mother have I come to realize just how difficult it must have been for her to manage a household of *eight* kids. Like so many mothers, she did the best she could. I reminded myself that she had married at the age of nineteen, when she was still a child herself.

My own experience has taught me that becoming able to forgive is one of life's most challenging and most rewarding mysteries. To forgive, after all, is to become *divine* in our humanity. The act is often blocked by our own precious ego, which would prefer to enforce its will on the world. The master ego is like the master attorney and accountant of the self and wants only to make sure all accounts are up to date and paid in full. It is the ego, too, that enforces the rule, "An eye for an eye, a tooth for a tooth." But it is the spirit, I believe, that says, "Love your enemies, bless them that curse you." Christ's words weren't telling us to be weak or accept persecution; they were telling us to look deeply into any evil or injustice done to us and then act in a radically different manner than we otherwise might. Forgiving is not the surrender or retreat of a weakling but an act that requires true courage.

Christ provided more than lyrical rules and aphorisms to his followers, however, for he completed these ideas with an unforgettable parable. After he said, "bless them that curse you, do good to them that hate you, and pray for them which despitefully use you, and persecute you," he continued, "That ye may be the children of your Father which is in heaven: for he maketh his sun to rise on the evil and on the good, and sendeth rain on the just and the unjust. . . . Be ye therefore perfect, even as your Father which is in heaven is perfect."

The use of the sun in these lines sheds the light of connectedness on all of mankind. The same sun that shines on you today is the same one that has shone on your ancestors since the beginning of time. And it will continue to shine—on your children, your grandchildren, and all your descendants—until the end of time. This is the very same sun that shone on Jesus, Moses, Buddha, Mahatma Gandhi, Mother Teresa, and Martin Luther King Jr. It is the same source of life for all of mankind, and it does not stop shining on anyone just because they do us wrong.

On a spiritual level, this image of the sun also symbolizes the light of the creator, which exists in all humans. We are, essentially, beings of light. As most of us know, it is one thing to experience ourselves or our loved ones as part of this light when things are going well, but it is a lot more difficult to see the same light in someone who has committed a terrible, seemingly unforgivable act against us. Yet, if it is at all possible for us to forgive them, that small yet boundless act opens us up to recognizing the divine spark within them and, by extension, within ourselves. This does not mean that a harmful deed is acceptable. The idea behind Christ's words is to engage in nonviolent action rather than violent reaction. For violence simply breeds more violence. Instead, we must have the courage to transform the situation with forgiveness.

WEEKLY EXERCISE

Forgive and Forget

Our first exercise is a tactile one. I am sure you have already done this while reading this chapter, but take a look now at your *index* finger. Take note of its straightness or crookedness and whether your Jupiter finger is marked by any outstanding markings such as a cut or wart. Now return to your journal and write down your sense of why these markings are there (if at all) and describe your index finger in the terms laid out in this chapter. For example, "My *index* finger is *long* and *curved*. This means that I am self-confident but can be overly cautious."

Next, sit quietly and with each hand touch the tip of your index finger to the tip of your thumb, making a circle, palm open. If it is comfortable, sit cross-legged or with your legs straight out in front of you and rest the back of your hands on your legs. You are now sitting like a yogi or guru, and that is appropriate, for as we discover our psychic selves, we become our own gurus. Take a deep breath. Breathe again, and as you release the breath, do so with this thought in mind: *I forgive myself for my limitations.* Breathe again, and as you exhale, breathe out whatever thought accompanied those negative aspects of your index finger, as in: *I forgive myself for being overly cautious.* Continue breathing, and each time you release a breath, release even more of the perceived limitations of self that have blocked your own experience of bliss. You may wish to repeat a certain phrase to facilitate this, such as: *I forgive myself for not loving myself in the past,* or *I forgive myself for all of my unloving behavior toward myself and others.*

When you feel the exercise is completed, say the words "thank you" aloud. Though it may sound strange, when we say these two simple words out loud, we are actively telling the unconscious that we have truly forgiven ourselves and therefore, are open to forgiving others.

The following exercises will require you to use your journal. I find that writing is deeply healing, especially in regard to healing *negative* feelings. In this instance, of course, we will use our index fingers to write.

First, write the names of the people who have hurt you and whom you cannot forgive. Then, write a short letter to each one, stating your feelings very openly. Be aware beforehand that you are not going to *send* these letters, you are going to *burn* them. Because of this, you can be completely honest about what you perceive to be the harm done to you. Then, take a moment to reread what you have written. Are there instances where you yourself had some responsibility or part in the perceived injustice? Please make a note of this in each case.

Once you have read through your letters and list, use care and safety and burn them. As you do so, pray that you will be able to let go of the pain and hurt. Watch your pain go up in flames as you release it to a higher power and breathe deeply while you say aloud, "*God bless the person/these people whom I cannot forgive. God grant me the grace to live as a woman/man of dignity and honor today. Thank you.*"

Finally, turn to a new page in your journal. Divide the page into three columns. In the first column, make a list of the people with whom you are *angry*. You need to forgive them and yourself. In the second column, next to those first entries, write down exactly why you are angry; be completely honest, expressing every negative thought that comes into your mind. Then, in the third column, *change your mind.* Do this by writing down *any* positive attributes the person you are angry with may have. Now that you have noted that these people in your life possess both negative and positive aspects, you have identified them as *human beings.* Once you have written this all out on paper, look back on it as the week progresses; notice how your level of indignation or acceptance vacillates in either direction, for I can promise you that if you are completely honest, it will.

Once you have completed this chart, you have already begun to *forgive yourself,* which is the second part of this exercise. Create a new three-column ledger, but this time, put yourself in the first column. And remember that your own emotions are as complicated as those of other people. You may be surprised at the contradictory feelings about yourself that this exercise brings forth. But understanding the paradox we all are will dramatically enrich your experience, for it ultimately enables you to *listen* to who you really are.

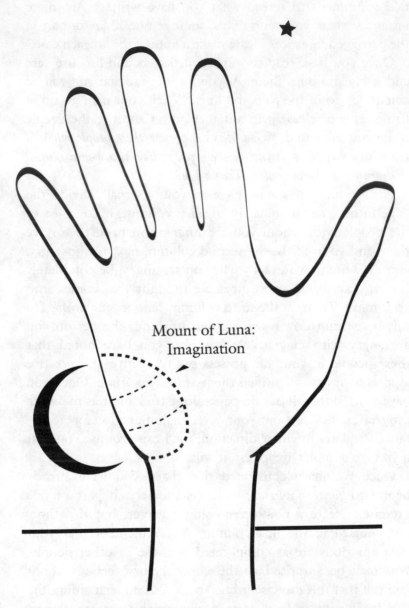

Mount of Luna:
Imagination

*Intuitive Messages, Dreams, and Our Deepest
Imagination Are Found on the Mount of Luna.*

THIRTEEN

Imagination: The Mount
of Luna

Intuitive messages, along with our dreams and imagination, often arise from the unconscious, and it is up to us to listen to those communications. The *Mount of Luna*, located on the outside of the hand directly across from the *Mount of Venus*, is the part of the hand that represents those unconscious aspects of ourselves that motivate and sustain our own unique vision and which enable us to be more authentic in our lives.

One of the many special moments in my career was when I met the surrealist painter Salvador Dali. Not only did he want to paint me, but he had so many *stars*, revealing a romantic, adventurous character, and *whorling* patterns, representing imagination, covering his *Luna mount* it made me dizzy. His mount was so *well-developed* it was no surprise that his extraordinary personality had found expression in great and dreamlike works of art.

A *well-developed* Luna mount can be as fleshy as the *Mount of Venus*, the seat of desire. The stronger and more *prominent* the Luna mount, the greater the imagination of its bearer.

Traditionally associated with the realm of the unconscious and the dream world, the Luna mount may also express a love of water, something I have often found in the hands of the fishermen and navigators I have read in the age-old fishing community I live in on the eastern tip of Long Island. And an *outward curve* on a well-developed Luna mount expresses this love of water most specifically.

Before time existed, the Roman moon goddess, Luna, the eternal Great Mother, drifted alone on the primal sea of chaos. In order to escape her own loneliness, Luna decided to create a world of form and order, and she is credited with establishing the physical world.

This idea, that a female moon goddess was responsible for the creation of the world, was not unique to the ancient Romans. The early Egyptian priests called the moon the "Mother of all that is," while the Persians used their word for mother, *Metra,* to name the moon. *Menos,* a Greek word, meant both moon and generative power. Similarly, the Polynesians called the moon the Creatress Hina, or the first woman. For the Sioux Indians, "the old woman who never dies" is how the moon was known, and the Iroquois dubbed her the Eternal One. Finally, the early Christians tried to discourage the Romans from worshipping Luna by saying that they were crazy to do so, and this is where the word *lunatic* stems from.

In each case, these myths or beliefs are a conscious attempt to understand and thereby describe the mysterious intelligence that sustains the rhythms of life. On the individual level, the Luna mount represents our relationship to our own personal unconscious, or "id," as Freud would have it, as well as our relationship with Jung's "collective unconscious," the vast psychic storehouse of all mankind.

The unconscious and the dream world are closely related to our own personal memories as well as those memories related to the collective unconscious. Because of this, the Luna mount may be divided into three parts, which delineate different aspects of our relationship to memory. The fleshier each section of the mount is, the more accessible will be the area of memory to which it refers. The first section, located at the *top* of the mount, is the repository of our childhood memories; the second section, located in the *middle* of the mount, indicates ancestral memories. If this section of your mount is well-developed, you most likely revere memories or stories relating to your family history, and you probably have a talent for genealogical studies. Lastly, a well-developed third section, located at the *bottom* of the mount, indicates a more widespread interest in memory and a possible talent for the study of ancient history, archeology, or philosophy.

Most likely, there is an area, sometimes more than one, on your Luna mount that is more developed than the others. But *any* well-developed area indicates an active unconscious life. Even if we do not consciously know it, the proof that our unconscious voice wants to be heard can be found in the symbols and signs of our dreams.

Sleep studies have proven the wonderful reality that during sleep, our access to the powers of the brain's right hemisphere is heightened. This same access is often diminished during our waking hours due to the restrictions our logical mind places on us. What researchers found is that experiments that tested telepathy were performed successfully while test individuals were sound asleep. The fact is, telepathy (communication from one mind to another by means other than those of our regular sensory channels) occurs when we allow ourselves to process information as it enters our minds without filter or censor. In other words, it is the transmittal of information by psychic means.

Dr. Montague Ullman, a psychiatrist who performed tests at a dream clinic during the 1950s, would wait until a sleeping subject began to dream (an act made obvious by rapid eye movement, or REM) and would then test the theory of telepathy by making a telephone call and instructing the "sender," who was several miles away, to open an envelope that had been sent and which contained a "target" picture. The sender would then concentrate on the target picture, and attempt to transmit his or her thoughts to the sleeper. Although many sleepers upon waking reported dreams that had nothing to do with those target pictures, several reported dreams that included images that so closely resembled the pictures it was startling.

In the earliest days of the twentieth century, J. W. Dunne, a mathematics professor and scientist, found that he'd begun to dream of events before they occurred. At first, his dreams consisted of simple, uncomplicated events, such as being chased by a horse. To his amazement, a few days later, he was indeed chased by a horse. Soon, he began to have other dreams that foretold global events, such as the eruption of Mount Pelée in 1902. That eruption destroyed the city of Saint Pierre, which was the main trading center of the island of Martinique, and killed some forty thousand people.

Over time, Dunne met others whose dreams contained this kind of foreknowledge, and his skepticism shifted into intense curiosity. He began to keep dream records, and after in-depth discussions with others about the content of his and their dreams, he proved to himself that the mind can indeed expand beyond the boundaries of time and space during sleep. This eventually led him to develop a theory which he called *temporal serialism*. Temporal serialism was, in effect, an argument that posited the idea that a fourth dimension existed. At the heart of this theory was the notion that the *passage* of time itself had to take time, therefore, if time takes time there must be a time outside of time. In other words, most of our lives, our waking hours, are spent inside of time. It is only when we are asleep, then, that we are able to break free of time as we know it and experience the deeper dimension of dream time, or time outside of time. This place of vast freedom and limitless time is where we may truly be in touch with our psychic selves.

How then may we bring the qualities of dream time into our daily lives? We may begin by analyzing our own Mount of Luna. An *overdeveloped* Luna mount reveals an extroverted character, which belongs to those of us who tend to be restless and desire escape from the mundane realities. An *underdeveloped* mount indicates a calm demeanor and a realistic personality whose emotions may not easily be expressed. Luna mounts that are marked with a *star* often belong to adventurous, charismatic individuals (like Mr. Dali) who tend to love travel. A deeply romantic streak often accompanies this sense of adventure and wanderlust. If a *cross* is found at the Mount of Luna, it reveals a boisterous personality and you may tell tall tales in an effort to impress others. A *grille* on the Luna mount indicates an overactive imagination, which may cause nervousness and tension, and so easy success in practical matters may elude you.

A *square*, which sometimes symbolizes knowledge, is rarely seen in this area, since it is in direct opposition to the imagination itself, but is found on the Luna mount of those few individuals with extremely grounded personalities. An *island* on the Luna mount, conversely, reveals such an isolated nature that an imaginary world may be much more inviting to you than the temporal one; you may have the ability to create something unusual in an artistic field. Similarly, a *dot* in this area does not represent a shock of some kind (its usual meaning); instead it suggests a craving to escape the routine, though there may be no other goal in mind.

Lastly, a *triangle* on the Mount of Luna indicates a proclivity for clairvoyance and an abundance of psychic gifts.

Many people with well-developed Luna mounts have sought creative expression in literature and the arts, as well as in the sciences. Most of us have been taught that we are either creative or not and that we simply cannot have it all, so we often wonder what life is like on the other side of the fence. For those of us with underdeveloped Luna mounts, the mysterious, intuitive world may seem inaccessible to us. But it is already inside each of us and is waiting to be discovered.

When I was taking my morning walk not long ago, I noticed the clouds in the sky, glanced at my watch, and realized that I had only thirty minutes before I needed to head home to get my kids off to school and my husband to work. So I had a choice to make: I could take a more direct and less interesting route home, or I could take the more arduous and more beautiful route by the dunes on the beach. I began to take the easier walk, but then I hesitated. An inner nudge urged me toward the beach. As I approached the shore, it began to rain, and as I walked on, a rainbow appeared over the water.

To my mind, that rainbow was the reward I received for listening to my inner voice. Logic may indeed dictate a certain course of action that promises ease and convenience, but if we listen to our inner voice when it urges us to take a road less traveled, we may encounter something so much better than ease and convenience—a rainbow! It is the unexpected surprises in life that stir our imaginations and create inspiration in a way that logic simply cannot.

Albert Einstein once said, "The intellect has little to do on the road to discovery. There comes a leap in consciousness, call it intuition or what you will, and the solution comes to you and you don't know how or why." I completely agree with Mr. Einstein: no matter what type of Luna mount you possess, intuition and creativity are yours for the listening.

I was thrilled when the time came to work on this chapter, for the simple act of listening to the creative in ourselves is at the very heart of a fully-realized, psychic life. For some of us, an *intuition* (or *psychic*, or *Mercury*) line already exists on our palm, bordering the inside portion of the Luna Mount, starting near the wrist and slanting vertically toward the Mercury finger. My own intuition line is as strong and deep as my other major lines, and my Luna mount is well-developed, which reveals my willingness to delve into the world of the imagination and my commitment to understanding my dreams. The fact that many of us do *not* possess an intuition line does not mean we cannot develop psychic abilities; it may mean, instead, that we are *not* in the habit of listening to our intuitive voice, and this is something that we all may cultivate.

As mentioned earlier, I ask each client to write down the questions he or she would like to have answered during the reading and to place this piece of paper under his or her pillow the night before the reading. I often dream about and visualize the new client in my dreams and frequently get strong intuitive messages as to why that client is coming to see me.

One night, I dreamed of a female client, whom I had yet to meet, and I dreamed that she had a prominent scar. Victoria arrived at my office the next morning, and I met a lovely woman of forty-seven with clear, unblemished skin. As I studied her palms, I was struck by the vast difference between them. Victoria's *dominant* hand was powerful and nearly flawless: no *islands, chains,* or *descending branches* marked any area; her major lines were deep and balanced; the *vertical lines* beneath her *Mercury* (or *pinky* finger) and a strong *intuition line* indicated a substantial healing ability. Victoria's nondominant hand, however, was the opposite: each major line had been claimed by *chains* and *islands,* indicating depression, illness, or loss; her *life* and *head* lines were connected, suggesting a dependence on the approval of others; finally, her *well-developed* Luna mount was crossed by a very large *scar.*

One look at Victoria's hands told me that she had come into the world with many obstacles and challenges, which were indicated by the markings on her nondominant hand. The presence of the intuition line and the well-developed Luna mount on her dominant hand revealed her inherent psychic abilities and her capacity to take the risks needed to successfully combine creativity and fulfillment. Her *knotty* fingers also emphasized her creative capabilities.

"You have overcome so much in your life," I said. "The scar on your Luna mount tells me that you have had more than your share of emotional pain and that you came into the world to overcome this pain. Your dominant hand contains gifts of healing and psychic ability; it is a hand of pure, unfolding trust. I see that you have been married . . . twice?" Victoria nodded. There were two significant *breaks* on her *life* line. "And you have had two near-death experiences?" She nodded again. "I was in a car accident. My left side is completely scarred." Victoria then showed me her forearm, which had been operated on four times. "Last year," she added, "I was diagnosed with breast cancer." She showed me the top of the scar on her chest where her left breast had been removed.

I knew nothing more about her life than what she had just told me, but I said, "Each time you had one of these near-death experiences, you left one of your husbands. Is that true?" She took a sharp breath. "I never thought of it that way," she said, "but you're right. Those relationships were not healthy." "So it took extreme circumstances to convince you to listen to your own intuition," I continued. "I sense that you are a person who knows much about others and that you are a healer in many ways." Victoria nodded again and told me that she worked with other cancer patients and that this seemed to benefit her own healing process. After she lost her breast, Victoria had decided to live her life moment by moment. "And yet," I said gently, "you still do not trust your own intuitive feelings."

Victoria looked as if she might burst into tears. I knew this was the reason she had come to see me. "How can I, Donna? I would like to have another relationship, but I keep picking the wrong men! I had to almost die twice before being able to get free of them! It's true, I feel things so deeply—even in my dreams. But how do I know if a man is right for me? I've been wrong so much in the past!"

I took a deep breath before responding. "Victoria," I began, "all that has happened in your life has led you to this very place. Hundreds of women have asked me that exact question, 'How do I know if a man is right for me?' But that is *not* the question they are really asking. What you are asking is, 'How do I learn to trust my own instincts?' And my answer is always the same: By listening to yourself. When you listen to what your intuition tells you the instant you feel it, your response will almost always be the correct one. Too often we ignore our gut and let the intellect take over, and we allow it to convince us of things we really don't believe. That is when we get into trouble. The more you practice listening to those little nudges inside you, the closer you will come to knowing your choices are right."

Listening to ourselves seems so simple, but as Victoria's story demonstrates, believing what we hear can be extremely difficult. I would have loved to have read the palm of Ralph Waldo Emerson, for I have no doubt that his own *intuition* line was as deep and strong as his other major lines. In an 1883 essay he wrote, "Dreams have a poetic integrity and truth. . . . They seem to us to suggest a certain abundance and fluency of thought not familiar to the waking experience." While Victoria's dreams obviously made impressions on her waking consciousness, she did not believe them any more than she believed her waking voice. In time, I knew she would begin to trust herself, both consciously and unconsciously, for her hands were certain proof of that.

In my own life, I came to understand the power and truth of dreams when I moved to New York City so many years ago. I was between apartments and staying with a new friend in exchange for baby-sitting her two-year-old son. Alone in the apartment one night, I had an unforgettable dream: I was being woken up by an older man who was trying to get into bed with me. "Get out of my room!" I shouted. The man said, "I could have a gun!" Without missing a breath, I shouted even louder, "You'll have to shoot me then, because you're not getting into my bed!" I must have yelled so loudly I woke myself up, for when I did awake, I saw a man leaving the apartment, the door wide open behind him. It had not been a dream at all!

For days, I battled with myself about whether or not I had actually been dreaming. The open door seemed proof that I had not, yet I certainly did not want to accept reality. Regardless of my conscious state, I had listened to my higher self, the part of me that always tells me the correct thing to do if I am listening, and so I had remained strong and in control. I later found out that the man lived right next door and had let himself into my friend's unlocked apartment.

Listening to my inner voice in times of crisis and in everyday life has become a priority for me. I cannot stress how important it is that each of us do the same, for it is our intuitive, rather than our conscious, self that never fails to rescue, advise, and reward us.

Not long ago, I met a striking young woman in her midtwenties named Olive who had recently been diagnosed with the HIV virus. She arrived at my office, and as I looked at her hand, I was relieved to see no signs of ill health, no *broken* lines, *islands,* or *dots* anywhere. I did, however see a *firm, well-developed Mount of Venus,* indicating a passionate nature and strong sexuality. Olive also had a well-developed *Mount of Luna,* which revealed her significant creative abilities. Her *oval-shaped* hands revealed a certain sensuality and the ability to attract many lovers. I told her that she was doing very well and that I saw no signs of illness or loss; in fact, I saw a woman with a strong, long life ahead of her.

"What else do you see?" she demanded. I continued, "You are interested in other areas of the future, aren't you? Such as marrying a man and having children?" Olive said yes. "But this is not as important to you as you think," I heard myself say. "What do you mean?" she pressed. I wasn't certain of the meaning behind the words I had just uttered myself until I closed my eyes and waited for the pictures to appear behind them. I saw Olive dancing a ballet and then happily dancing naked on a stage. Finally, I saw her crying. I opened my eyes and told her what I saw.

Olive couldn't believe I saw these aspects of her life: she had been trained in classical ballet and presently worked as an exotic dancer in Las Vegas. As for the tears, she had told her parents about her HIV status but was afraid to tell her fiancé's family. "I don't want anyone to treat me differently, or feel sorry for me," she said. "And I don't want anyone to judge me. *I had this dream* about everyone at my wedding, where my boyfriend's family got up and took him and rushed out of the church, leaving me all alone."

My heart ached for Olive, and I reached once more for her hand. "Your shame about contracting this virus has interfered with your dream life," I said softly. "You are terribly anxious about being judged by others." "Now tell me something I don't know!" Olive said, and we both laughed. "The truth is," I said, "you came into this world to be creative and not to be scared of the process of discovery in any area, there aren't many people who would feel comfortable dancing naked in front of other people! But your hand tells me that you are talented in other arts as well. If you feel good about being a dancer, dance and enjoy it. Transform these negative feelings about your health status into something positive. Face your life head-on and know that you have something to share with other young people, so they might avoid finding themselves in the predicament you are now in. Judging from your own words, you are already in touch with your dreams, so begin to keep a journal and ask your spirit guide for help. What you dream may help others. I sense that you are here on earth to do wonderful things, but that it is up to you to take the right action."

Olive did get married, though she chose not to tell her in-laws about her HIV status. She soon started speaking to kids in high schools about how to protect themselves from contracting the HIV virus, for her own infection was the result of unprotected sex. Olive started keeping a journal of her dreams, she later told me, and that is where the idea to talk to teens about HIV had come from. Since then, Olive's health has remained strong and she has begun to work with a researcher to understand HIV and childbearing issues.

Many of us may still be skeptical about listening to our dreams; we may have trouble believing that they may provide information essential to our daily, waking lives. To help us better understand this connection, I will tell a story that embodies these very ideas, a true story that is nearly five hundred years old. It was told to me by a kindly gentleman from Norfolk County, England.

I was traveling through the English countryside on vacation several years ago and decided to rest at the Church of Saint Peter and Saint Paul in Swaffham. While I sat and admired the church, the sexton introduced himself and offered a bit of history about the church and surrounding countryside. In no uncertain terms, he told me, this beautiful structure owed its existence to someone's dream.

During the fifteenth century, there was a tinker from Swaffham by the name of John Chapman. One night, Mr. Chapman had a powerful dream that bid him to travel to London and wait at a certain spot on London Bridge; if he waited there, he would meet someone who would change his life. The next morning, Chapman told his wife about the dream, but his wife just laughed at him.

The following night, he had the same dream. He told his wife, and she laughed again. The third night, he dreamt the same dream, but this time he chose not to tell his wife about it; instead, he went directly to London, where he stood on the particular spot on the bridge and waited. All day he stood on the bridge, but nobody approached him. He stood there a second day, unapproached by anyone once more. On the third day, he stood at the spot until just after darkness had settled, and at the moment he was about to lose all faith in the dream, a stranger approached him.

The stranger asked him why he had been waiting at this spot for so long, and Chapman told the stranger of his dream without mentioning where he was from. The stranger listened quietly until Chapman finished his story, and then the stranger laughed, just as his wife had. "Only fools believe that dreams mean anything. Why, just last night I had a dream where I was in some town called Swaff-ham. I dug under an apple tree next to an abandoned well and discovered a box of money."

Chapman was dumbstruck. He rushed home and began to dig under that apple tree. About three feet down he hit something—a chest full of gold and silver coins! In gratitude for his newfound wealth, Chapman made a large donation so that a new church could be built in Swaffham. If you ever find yourself in that part of the English countryside, be sure to visit the Church of Saint Peter and Saint Paul, where there is a stained-glass window that depicts the story of Mr. Chapman and his dream.

Chapman's story is truly remarkable. Though some people may choose to believe it is nothing more than a folktale, we can still believe that the treasure he unearthed is far more precious than mere gold and silver; it is the treasure of the boundless, unlimited richness of the human imagination. In dreams, we have infinite flexibility; we can bend and mold space and time at our mind's whim, and this freedom can greatly influence our waking life. In order to experience these benefits, however, we must first acknowledge the importance of our dreams. Rather than viewing our time asleep as a short rest from the daily activities of life, and our dreams as meaningless mental images and sensations, we should view sleep as a time in which our minds journey into a mysterious realm that is as essential to our well-being as our waking state. Just as Chapman realized the importance of his dream even though he did not understand it, we, too, can learn to listen to and value the images we experience in our dreams. I have never doubted for a moment that my dreams hold riches that are far more precious than gold and silver. Both Victoria and Olive struggled to embrace these very riches, and they ultimately found them within.

WEEKLY EXERCISE

Listening to Our Dreams

At the end of each day, try to remember Mr. Chapman's story; in doing so, you will automatically begin to honor your own dreams. Once you are comfortably settled in bed and are ready to drift off, meditate for a few moments, offering a prayer of gratitude for the good things the day offered. Even if nine thousand nine hundred and ninety-nine things went wrong, search your mind for the *one* thing that went right and be grateful for it. If you are hard-pressed to come up with something, be grateful for the very bed you are lying on. This may sound simplistic, but it will, in fact, prepare you to enter the sleep state in a positive and open manner.

With a feeling of wonder, you will enter the creative state of unconsciousness that is sleep, and you will find yourself engaged in a truly miraculous mental adventure. Remind yourself to remember what you dreamed about when you awaken. In order to achieve this, you may wish to leave a small notebook and pen on your nightstand; this way, as soon as you awaken in the morning or during the night you can easily jot down any images or fragments of dreams that remain with you. You will soon discover that dream recall is a talent that is easy to develop. Indeed, after a few months you will most likely recall three or four dreams each night.

The following meditation will help ease you comfortably and gradually into a receptive state of *listening*. I suggest putting it on audiocassette, so that you can actually hear these instructions spoken to you in your own voice.

Assume a comfortable position, sitting or lying down. Close your eyes and begin to breathe slowly and easily, becoming aware of your physical body as you do so. Allow yourself to feel grounded and centered. Breathe into every part of yourself, beginning with your feet, your legs, your hips . . . your entire body, all the way up to the top of your head. Gently massage your hands together, paying special attention to the Luna mount. Now take a moment to call out your own name. Become aware of the sound of your voice, and know that you are connecting to your deepest inner self.

In your mind's eye, take yourself on a journey through the atmosphere until you are sitting quietly by a body of water. It may be a lake, a stream, a pond, or an ocean—whatever appeals most to you. When you arrive, the mental image may be clear or it may be hazy. Do not judge it; simply be where you are. Permit yourself now to look into the water; whether your picture is hazy or clear, allow yourself to experience the sense of being close to a wonderful source in nature.

As you sit comfortably in this place, are there any sensations of sound nearby? Name them out loud. Do you see colors? Name them out loud as well. Whatever you see or hear—it may be your own breath—is perfect. Again, call out your own name, and continue to imagine yourself in this beautiful place.

When you are ready, ask to meet an entity, or being, who can guide you in spiritual matters. Shape your request as precisely as you can: 'I wish for the wisest being who has my best interests at heart to guide me.' Or, you may wish to ask your higher self to approach and guide you. Allow this being, or guide, to approach you from behind, *if that is comfortable, for your perception of energy is often clearer behind you than before you. (Perhaps this is why we often visualize a guardian angel hovering behind an individual.)*

Breathe deeply as you ask this entity to appear, and be aware of your feelings. What do you see and feel? Begin to notice your reactions at this moment—if you feel uncomfortable at any time, simply ask your guide to wait while you explore your reactions. Feel free to open your eyes at any time or adjust your physical position.

You may enter this state for many sittings and not be ready to truly embrace your guide with your total consciousness. When you are ready to do so, you may then interact with it. You may wish to ask for a visual image to accompany the entity, or you may name it, so that you will be able to recognize it in the future.

When you are ready, ask your entity what it might teach you or how it might guide you during this session. Ask your guide if there is a special place where or manner in which you might contact him or her. You may find it easy to imagine a dialogue, or you may see images rather than words. In time, you will find that the exchange is not *necessarily a verbal, conscious experience, but rather a deeper knowingness of your higher self.*

At the end of each session, thank the entity, or guide, that has come to you. Even if you have not perceived an actual presence, give thanks anyway, for I can assure you that a presence has been there; in time, your perception will deepen and you will become more aware.

Breathe deeply once more and become aware of the body of water again. Name yourself out loud, bringing your awareness back to the conscious state. When it is comfortable for you, open your eyes and shift your body. Allow yourself a few minutes to return to full consciousness. Softly rub your hands and fingers against each other, paying particular attention to your Luna mount as you do so, for your mount may now be so enlivened it may even tingle.

After fully emerging from this experience (and even while still in it), it is useful to write or audiotape what you see, feel, and hear; this act can help you to catch fleeting details and images that are fully formed in the dream state but rapidly fade as consciousness returns.

For some people, this exercise is relatively easy; at this stage of willingness, your guides enter consciousness very quickly. But for others, there are barriers even willingness cannot pass through and surrendering to the unconscious may take longer. In either case, allow yourself *three months* to become fully engaged with your higher self, for that is how long it takes before any *habit* becomes second nature.

Also remember to keep a pen and paper beside your bed so that you may make a habit of recording aspects of your dreams as well as various states of awareness. Your dreams will do the deeper work; all you need do is listen. In my view, my day's work is done when I approach my bed. When I lie down, I picture my higher power's hands above me, and into these I place my problems and worries, my joy and my gratitude—everything that weighs on me, both good and bad. Once I have done this, I may sleep in peace and will be receptive to the creative intuition that appears to us only in our dreams.

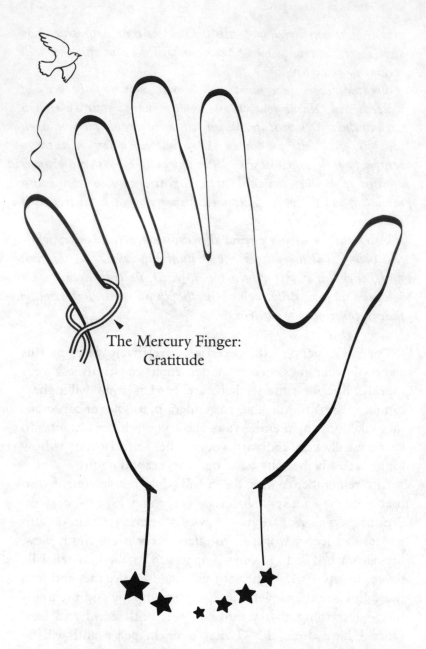

The Mercury Finger:
Gratitude

Understand Your Verbal Skills, Sense of Humor,
and Find Gratitude by Looking at Your Mercury Finger.

FOURTEEN

Gratitude: The Mercury Finger

The *Mercury* (or *pinky*) finger, which is so small in comparison to our other fingers, is largely responsible for revealing our communicative abilities. This finger is associated with verbal skill, and many successful singers, actors, and playwrights have long and well-formed pinky fingers; the longer the finger, the greater the ability to communicate with others.

The messenger of the gods to mortals, Mercury, flying on winged feet and straddling the mythic and mundane worlds, is the god of communication. Our Mercury finger reveals our ability to intuit, diagnose, and analyze situations, and indicates how skillful we are at adapting ourselves to the world around us.

The only finger that joins the hand at a low place, a very *low set* pinky is a sign that parental relationships may be unresolved and therefore the person with this type of pinky may experience complications in romantic interactions. These problems, however, may be ameliorated by addressing the unresolved issues we have with our parents.

The Mercury finger is also the most separate from the others; an isolated Mercury finger may literally indicate a state of apartness that would make intimate relationships difficult. However, this difficulty should be considered only in relationship to other elements of the hand. For example, an isolated pinky finger coupled with a well-developed Mount of Venus that is covered with grilles may indicate a preoccupation with sex over true intimacy. It is crucial to take the markings of the entire hand into account when deciphering information as it pertains to a specific individual.

If the Mercury finger is set evenly at the base and is not isolated and its *average* length reaches roughly two-thirds of that of the *Apollo* finger, you possess a healthy balance between your romantic and business lives.

A Mercury finger that is *longer* than this reveals that you are both persuasive and diplomatic and are able to get to the crux of any matter quickly. Often successful politicians or negotiators have this type of long pinky finger.

A *short* Mercury finger belongs to those of you who tend to be blunt and are able to win others over with your earnestness. If you have this type of pinky, you are likely to experience frequent nervous tension and stress, and you may not be attentive enough to your own needs.

A *crooked* Mercury finger reveals a rather cunning personality. Usually, both pinkies are crooked; if only one pinky is crooked (usually the left), it could mean that you have been let down in the past and find it nearly impossible to forgive and forget. Ironically, a *bent* pinky indicates that the bearer possesses healing abilities.

Lastly, here is a tip for all you soul seekers: when a person wears a *ring* on the Mercury finger, it reveals the very best the finger has to offer, a lively intellect and avid intuitiveness, often coupled with a vivacious sexuality.

You may wonder how the Mercury finger relates to gratitude; though small in size, it is mighty in meaning. Because of its inherent intuitive qualities, our pinky enables us to communicate from the highest level of ourselves. Communicating from our highest level—that is, openly, honestly, and directly—is the most important way we can express our own gratitude in life. By expressing our gratitude to those around us, we may change the lives of all involved, especially ourselves.

Earlier in my life, I often wished I could be somewhere else: when I was in San Francisco, I wanted to be in New York; when I was in Paris, I wanted to go to Madrid. I also wanted to be someone else too. My mind was riddled with thoughts that began with the phrase, "*If only . . .*" If only I had my parents' support; if only I had different traits; and so on. I was never satisfied with myself until I learned to live with gratitude *in the moment.*

When I was twenty-three, I had an idea for a television show that would be called *The Loser Show.* This idea reflected how I viewed the world at that time: you were either a winner or a loser; life was black or white, happy or sad. The idea for the show was this: New York City is a twenty-four-hour town, full of real people with real stories to tell. Instead of actors, I wanted to use real people to communicate their struggles, and struggle they do. As we all know, people come to this city to make it big—become a Broadway star, a whiz kid in the stock market, a football player for the Giants. We have been led to believe that making it in New York means that we can make it anywhere. But what becomes of us after a few years of *not* making it big? I wanted the show to be about exactly that: the football player who injures his knee and eventually becomes a hairdresser; the would-be star of stage and screen whose waitressing career has taken center stage.

The concept made it through the gates of one of the three big networks, and I had the chance to meet with a program director. He wanted to change the title of the show, but I refused; he wanted to hire a well-known host to take over the position I saw myself in, and I refused. To my mind, *any* changes he wanted to make were negative impositions rather than promising possibilities. By now, of course, you have already guessed the outcome of the meeting. I lost my opportunity to see my show make it to the screen. But you may still be wondering what this story has to do with gratitude.

The fact is, I identified with the losers. I, too, had big hopes that were never realized. Namely, I longed to be *Donna McCue, the greatest actress the world has ever known.* In reality, following my small part in *Midnight Cowboy*, I never landed another role, and I walked around with a life-is-a-half-empty-glass attitude. I was not grateful for my youth, my enthusiasm, my pretty face, or my healthy body. As with *The Loser Show*, when I did not get what I wanted, I quit. Then I would move on to something else, and when whatever it was I was interested in did not go my way, I quit again. I continued to repeat this pattern until I began to take my psychic gifts seriously and began to take jobs to support *it*, rather than the other way around.

As I began to honor the information that came through me during readings and meditation, my circumstances and my attitude began to change. I saw clients as evolving souls, not as winners or losers, and gratitude entered my life, changing it forever. When you are grateful, negativity dissolves and is replaced by a positive attitude, positive possibilities, and positive results. Twenty-five years later, I am proud to say that I now host my own television show, which is called *The Good News Show*. The show airs live, operating in a call-in format so that viewers may call and ask questions about their futures. The success of this show is entirely due to gratitude. Now, rather than viewing life as being about winning or losing, I concentrate on the *good* in everyone. On the air, I always remind viewers that the "good news" is *themselves*, and I always ask each caller to say something positive about the here

and now in their lives before leaping into a consideration of
the future.

Ultimately, I have learned that the more gratitude I have in
my own life, the more psychic I become. Grateful thoughts
accumulate and actually attract psychic energy, and this energy
field refines and transforms our consciousness so that we
might attract greater health, joy, success, and satisfaction.
Knowing how gratitude has changed my own life and that of
those around me, I have come to think of gratitude as a spiritual magnet that pulls success and abundance into our lives.

Speaking of magic, I once had the opportunity to read the
hands of an illusionist or magician. Thor was a handsome man
in his mid-thirties, five foot six inches tall with a muscular
body. His hands were *large,* which indicated his attention to
detail, and his fingers were *long* and *tapered,* revealing a sensitive, artistic side. His *Mercury* (or *pinky*) finger was extremely
long, almost the length of his *ring* finger. That pinky finger let
me know that Thor was able to get to the crux of any matter
and resolve it quickly and successfully. His *life* and *head* lines
were widely separated, revealing courage, impetuousness, and
self-reliance, and his *long* Jupiter (or *index*) finger indicated
that Thor's was a domineering, egocentric personality, which
was perfect for performing magic tricks!

"The bigger the hand," I said, "the better attention to
detail. With your tapered fingers, did you ever think of
another career, like being a doctor or surgeon, for example?"
Thor smiled broadly. "I can't believe you said that. That's
what I went to college to do. But I've been interested in
magic since I was a little kid, though I never thought I could
make a career out of it."

Once he started to make money performing magic at
nightclubs and parties, Thor came to feel that he would
"perform more healing doing this than taking out a kidney."
I did not disagree, for Thor's chosen profession obviously
allowed him a creative way to communicate with others.

"You must be grateful for a career that makes people happy and joyful," I said. He responded to my words with a big smile, and then reached behind my ear and presented me with the quarter he had magically found there.

Intuitive reason, like magic, exists beyond our everyday understanding. The demands of the mundane world further our opportunities to experience the divine that exists in the intuitive realm.

Alissa was thirty-two, and her difficult life became even harsher as the result of the early deaths of two of her loved ones. A dear friend of hers asked me to consult with the heartbroken and hopeless Alissa, who had become so apathetic she had stopped eating and spent most of her day watching television. When I looked at her hand, I saw a *love* line marked by a few *descending branches,* which clearly indicated disappointment in romantic relationships. Alissa also had two significant *dots* on her hand, one on her *heart* line and one on her *Mount of Venus.* There was no question that she had experienced shock and trauma and that love was Alissa's most problematic area. Her *long* fingers, however, attested to her reliability. Below her *low-set, isolated* finger of *Mercury,* which further revealed her troubled history with relationships, I noticed the certain lines on the edge of her hand, which indicated she would have three husbands.

"Three!" she shouted, clearly upset by this news. "I've already lost two!" Both of her husbands were fishermen who had died at sea, she explained. Her first husband had been lost at sea, and her second had been murdered by another fisherman miles from shore. Alissa felt that her life was cursed, and she wept openly. She had lost these two men within seven years, the second when she was barely thirty. "I don't believe in curses," I said, "but I do believe that God has a plan for each of us. Even though we cannot see it, ⟨⟩ do make choices along the way. One of those choices is to see the good in any situation—even if it seems like a completely bad situation."

I was not, of course, trying to tell Alissa to be grateful for the deaths of her husbands. As a fellow human being, I ached for her loss and for the loss of these young men, but as a psychic, I understood that our souls make a sacred contract before we come into this world and that the fulfillment of this contract, though it may bring us pain and suffering, is our only true route to peace and happiness. I advised Alissa to consider the choices she had made in marrying both of these men, each of whom had, I intuited, his own struggle with destructiveness— one had a drinking problem and had beaten Alissa, while the other had been unfaithful.

Wide-eyed, Alissa admitted that what I said was true, and in a meek voice, she revealed that while her husbands were alive, she had sometimes wished they were both dead. It became clear to me that her own sense of guilt was destroying the possibility of a happy existence for her. We both took a deep breath. "Alissa," I said, "you are faced with another choice: you can go on blaming yourself, or you can look for the good in this situation." We discussed how each of her husbands had provided for her by leaving behind life insurance policies that supported her enough that she would be able to devote her time to volunteer work. By doing this, she was able to give back to other people, such as the concerned friend who had called me, the care she obviously needed to cultivate for herself. At the end of our meeting, Alissa realized that much more good had come out of these sorrowful experiences than she had ever considered. She was still young enough to marry again, and her involvement with her community allowed her to see that there were men other than fishermen available, and for this alone, Alissa said, she was deeply grateful: the idea of eating one more piece of fish

hich still crowded her freezer) is what had finally caused
er to lose her appetite.

Finding gratitude within ourselves after loss, disappointment,
or illness is one of life's most difficult lessons, yet it is also a
great opportunity for all of us to reach a new level of understanding.

Giselle and her husband wanted to have a baby so badly
that she had seen enough doctors and specialists to staff her
own fertility clinic. As a last resort, she came to see me,
demanding that I see in her future what her heart so badly
yearned for.

I gently shifted the responsibility for her own life back to
her and softly stated that I could only tell her what I truly saw.
Giselle's hands were *knotty*, each finger attesting to a wonderful combination of creativity and practicality. Pointing out her
childbearing lines to her, located below her *short*, somewhat
crooked Mercury finger on the outside of the hand, I noted
that I saw six such lines. Her short pinky revealed Giselle's
blunt nature and stressed-out condition. One of Giselle's
hands had a crooked pinky, which indicated that she would
have problems letting go of previous disappointments.

"I've already had three miscarriages," she said slowly. "I
can't believe I could possibly have even one, much less three,
more pregnancies." She continued to shake her head as I told
her that this was a very real possibility and that the children
would not necessarily be *biologically* hers. Unable to accept
this information, Giselle ended our session and left abruptly.

Eight months later, I ran into Giselle in New York City. She
was walking down Fifth Avenue pushing a stroller big enough
to hold three beautiful Chinese babies with pink ribbons in
their hair. Giselle smiled proudly. "Are they triplets?" I asked
excitedly. "No," she said, "but remember what you told me
about being willing to love three more kids? Just look at how
precious they are!" Giselle was truly beaming. "Do you see

anything different about me?" "You look happy," I s[...] observing that she looked rosier and a bit rounder all over. [...] am," she blurted out excitedly, "and I'm pregnant!"

Giselle explained that she had become pregnant as soon as she returned home from China with her new children. After *sixteen* years of trying to have kids on her own, she had been blessed with this magical change in circumstances. To my mind, the magic in this story is that Giselle was able to continue opening her heart after losing, not once but three times, what she wanted so much. Giselle went on to say that as soon as she met the tiny Chinese girls, she was so grateful for the opportunity to love them that she adopted all three. "You planted the seed, Donna, by telling me that I could love more than one child." She rubbed her belly and went on, "And now, I'm going to have the little boy that I've always dreamed of."

Before we parted, I took Giselle's hand once more. A *seventh* child line had indeed appeared, indicating that Giselle's dream would now become reality. Life is indeed magical.

Mercury, the "messenger of the gods," came to symbolize the great power of communication between the secular world of mankind and the divine world inhabited by the gods. In fact, the word "communicate" comes from the Latin word *communicatus*, which means to "make common." As such, communication is the power to overcome the gaps that exist between separate entities. To live in the world as a human being is to live in a world of divisions. First, there is the division between ourselves and everyone else. We come to believe, as individuals, that we cannot experience what another experiences. However, we are born in the blissful state in which we and the world around us are one. It is only as we grow that we become aware of the separateness between "me" and the rest of the world.

As we grow, we also develop the ability to use language. This communicative ability enables us to share what we experience with others and lets others share their experience with us. Ultimately, this is how human culture is created and how we learn to live in harmony with one another. With the ability to communicate, however, comes the ability to lie or deceive. This vice is usually revealed by a *crooked* Mercury finger and sometimes is expressed by an actual injury to this finger.

Dominick was not a client of mine but rather was someone I met at a Christmas party several years ago. I had written a script for a television show, and a woman named Tine, a producer, had expressed interest in it. She had invited me to her Christmas party, and I was having a wonderful time, surrounded by delicious food and warm, friendly people. I was immersed in conversation with Tine, when a gentleman named Dominick interrupted our dialogue. "I hear you're a psychic," he said. "So what are the winning lottery numbers for this week?"

I told him that I wasn't that kind of psychic. In the next room, some guests were watching a Knicks game. "Yeah, well, what about the game? Who's gonna win?" he demanded. "Sorry, Dominick, " I explained, "I'm an intuitive who gives people insight about life by looking at their hands. If you want to know which basketball team to bet on, maybe you should call one of those nine hundred numbers." "Well," he replied, "if you can't pick the numbers or know who's gonna win the game, what good are you?" Neither mortified Tine nor I responded, and Dominick disappeared into the next room.

I didn't see him again until about three hours later, when I was getting ready to leave. He approached me again. "So you read palms?" He thrust his hand at me and said, "Give it your best shot." I told him that I didn't work while I was socializing, and that if he seriously wanted a reading, I'd leave a business card with him so that he could call for an appointment.

"Are you afraid that what you tell me is gonna be wro Dominick asked, then proceeded to take out a roll of bills fi his pocket and start to peel them off in front of a roomful people. "What do you charge? A hundred? Two? Three?"

Dominick was beginning to embarrass both Tine and myself. When it became clear that he was not going to stop his behavior, I said, "Dominick, I'll make you a deal. I'll give you a reading, but you don't have to give me any money. The next time you pass by a church you take that three hundred dollars and put it in the poor box." He agreed and then in a loud voice stated, "Okay, let's go, right here, right now."

I took his hand and closed my eyes. "Dominick," I said softly, "we can't do the reading here because your wife will hear about your girlfriends." Other guests laughed, but for the first time, Dominick had nothing to say. He followed me to a small study, and we sat down. Aside from everything else his hand might say about him, the fact that his right *pinky* was *missing* said it all. "Your poor pinkie, what happened?" I asked, but he waved the question away. "No big deal. I was a kid, playing with firecrackers, you know."

I "just knew" that he was lying. I looked then at his left hand, where his remaining pinky was severely *crooked*. "Did something happen to your pinky?" I asked. "You're the psychic, you tell me!" he replied. I noted that his palm was marked with several *scars*, and because they were located on his *life* line, I knew he had had more than one near-death experience. But he denied this. In fact, he denied everything I said during the session. When I said he had been in trouble with the law, he denied it. When I saw that he was the father of four children, he said he only had two.

With each denial, however, he grew increasingly quiet. At the end of the reading, he said I was completely wrong about everything, and he left in a hurry. I watched as he sought out his wife and quickly left the party. The next day, Tine called to apologize for Dominick's behavior. I assured her that it

been an interesting experience for me and that I was still
ndering about his missing pinky. "Oh, he's a wiseguy, you
now, a small time mobster. He grew up with my husband,
and he likes to come to our parties so he can hang out with
Hollywood types. My husband told me that he lost his finger
when he lied to some big shot in the mob. They cut it off to
teach him a lesson."

Though this is an extreme example, Dominick's career was
sorely hampered by his poor communication skills. He was a
compulsive liar. His missing pinky finger spoke this truth louder
than any words might have. I began to pray for Dominick then,
grateful that my life had been spared the unfortunate circumstances that had so obviously transformed his.

In the preceding chapter, I suggested that you end each day
with a feeling of gratitude. Every morning, I also begin the
day with a prayer of gratitude. As I listen to the sounds of the
household waking up, I am grateful for the simplest truths of
my life: for my boys, who are healthy and strong; for my husband, who works so hard and who always goes out of his way
to help others.

The other day, it was raining and the kids were still at
school. The house was quiet, and I built a fire in the fire-
place. As I lay on the couch, Lucky, my cat, jumped onto my
belly and purred loudly and fell asleep. The house was warm
and quiet, and as I watched the crackling fire, I was filled
with immense gratitude for that perfect moment.

Practicing Gratitude

When I was a child, at the breakfast table both of my parents would bite into a piece of toast and say, "*Mmmmm,* this is the best piece of toast I have ever had." Early on, it was a private joke between them, but they finally explained its origin: it was what Jack Benny said when he ate a piece of toast. The explanation made us kids think that our parents were even crazier than we had thought they were, but I have since learned that Mr. Benny was so popular because he expressed gratitude and good feeling no matter what the situation was, no matter how plain or dry the toast was, and that is why people loved him so. We can all learn something wonderful from that simple message.

This week's exercise, then, is very simple. First, make a piece of toast. As you bite into it, tell yourself that this is the best piece of toast you've ever had. Take note of the position of your *pinky* finger as you eat. Is it crooked or straight? A crooked pinky indicates your sense of cunning, and a straight pinky reveals your balanced nature. If you observe carefully, you will see that even the small, often overlooked Mercury finger plays a key role in every gesture the hand engages in.

As you complete this exercise, you will realize that everything you have just told yourself is true. Magically, life itself is that simple. During each moment, we have a choice about how we experience our lives; gratitude, then, is a choice we make to see things differently.

If we stop and think for a moment, it becomes clear to us that life itself is totally gratuitous. Nobody ever willed themselves into existence, and when it comes time to die, no one can will even one extra heartbeat. If we embrace this idea, we

...at life and everything in it is a gift. Our families and ...ds, the sunshine that falls on our faces, and the air mole-...es that fill our lungs—these are all gifts that we so often ...ake for granted. By practicing gratitude, however, we increase our appreciation for these simple aspects of our lives.

This change of focus will change the quality of our lives. Take the toast idea and expand upon it; apply it to other areas of your everyday existence. Your world will begin to feel fuller, more vital, more alive. The most wonderful thing about gratitude is, we can practice it anytime and anywhere.

Now that we have discussed each finger, we can consider all of them in these next exercises of gratitude: Look at your *thumb,* and say a prayer of gratitude for the people closest to you. Name five people or things whose presence in your life you are grateful for. In my case and at this time, I thank God for my husband, Larry, my sons, Danny and Alex, my coauthor, Stacey, and my agent, Joanna.

Next, look at your *index* finger, the pointing finger. Be grateful for those who use this finger to enrich our lives, such as teachers, doctors, and administrators. They need our support as much as we need theirs, so pick five names of mentors who have enriched your life and say a prayer of gratitude for each.

The *middle* finger, the tallest finger, reminds us of our leaders. Our gratitude to our president, to leaders in industry, business, and religion, should be acknowledged. Again, choose five and pray that God's guidance continues to touch their lives so they may lead us with truth and grace.

The *ring* finger is also the hand's weakest finger, as any piano teacher will attest. As such, it should remind us to pray for those who are in need. It also reminds us to be grateful for the abundance in our own lives. Take a few moments to think of five things you are grateful for and to pray for five people whose lives are lacking.

Lastly, our *little* finger, the smallest finger
remind us of our gratitude for the small things i
flowers, the sun, and the air we breathe. Each of
of every thought, word, and action in our lives.
breathe in life's goodness and be grateful for the gift
itself. Each time you look at your pinky finger, say "tl.
you" to yourself, and you will soon notice the flow of po
tive energy into your life. In fact, why not start a new trend
by tying a pink string around your pinky finger. When someone asks you what the string is for, you can say that it is there
to remind you of all you are grateful for in life, including
them.

Finally, here is yet another simple yet powerful exercise in
gratitude, which you can rely on anytime and anywhere:
when someone close to you does something that makes you
angry, pause a moment before reacting. Look at your *pinky*
finger, and imagine that the person is suddenly and forever
gone from your life; your anger will immediately subside and
be replaced with love. You will see that person for what they
are, a magical gift.

And do not hesitate to use this same technique on yourself. The next time you are dissatisfied with yourself, take a
deep breath and try to imagine what life would be like if you
had never existed. Think of the positive effects that you have
had in this world and on the people around you. There is an
ancient spiritual law that promises the following: the more
you are grateful for, the more you will be given.
Remembering that our littlest finger embodies this simple yet
profound idea, we are able to look with new appreciation at
the promise of our lives that is mapped out before us in the
lines and markings of the rest of our hand.

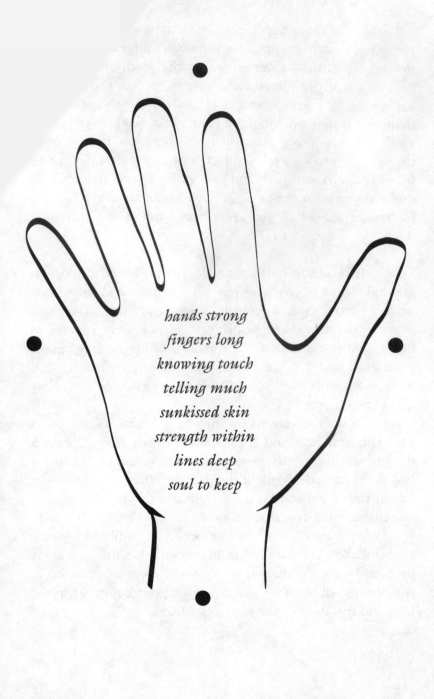

hands strong
fingers long
knowing touch
telling much
sunkissed skin
strength within
lines deep
soul to keep

FIFTEEN

Your Fate Is in Your Hands

Every day we make hundreds of choices. And each and every decision can result in a profound change in our lives, whether we are conscious of this or not. So I want to leave you with one last story that illustrates the incredible power of fate itself. It begins with the ringing of my telephone in the middle of a warm summer night several years ago. On the other end of the line was Joe, a client I had known for more than two years. Though I usually saw him in person during daylight hours, I heard his shaky voice and I knew that fate was interceding and I needed to wake up and offer Joe my help.

Joe was a highly successful computer engineer. Though he had grown up in the east, he had moved to California's Silicon Valley to pursue his career. Knowledgeable and dedicated, his most important work resulted in programming that significantly contributed to the Internet as we know it today. Soon after this success, he moved back east to start his own high-tech company and pursue other interests. One of those interests included a study of crystals and radionics (the subtle gy nature exerts over the human body's constitution), d it was over this hobby that we met. Joe called one day nd initiated a discussion about the forces that infused quartz crystals, which led to his asking questions about what forces I thought were behind intuition.

At our first consultation, I took Joe's hands in my own. His hands were *small*—indicating that he had big plans for his life. His *fate* line was absolutely striking; it was *long, deep,* and *continuous.* It was evident that here was a man whose intention to make his life and career outstanding would succeed. Because the line began near the base of the hand, it was obvious that he had known what he wanted to do with his life at a very early age. Also, his fate line was *straight* and without *breaks.* It ended at the *head* line, which told me that his mental abilities were quite impressive.

Joe immediately asked me several questions about his business dealings and seemed quite surprised by some of the answers I gave him. They must have been correct, because he continued to seek my advice on a regular basis, and a deep bond developed between us. Then he called at two A.M. It was obvious that he had just been through a traumatic experience and that he needed someone to help sort it out. After I suggested we take a few deep breaths together, Joe calmed down and I was able to ask him what had happened.

Apparently, the day had begun uneventfully. Joe had gone to his office to take care of his usual business. He did leave the office somewhat early, however, because he had ordered a limousine to take him to the airport that evening. After packing for his trip, Joe waited for his limo to arrive. He always used the same limousine service, he told me, and always asked for Paul, the same driver. Paul had proven utterly reliable and was also punctual, no matter the weather.

That day, Joe looked at his watch and realized that Paul was five minutes late. Then he was ten minutes late. Twenty minutes later, Paul had still not arrived. Joe finally called the limo service and was told that the car had been dispatche good time but that there was a new driver, by the name William, behind the wheel. Paul had apparently asked for th night off; he had been the tenth caller on a radio show and had won two concert tickets. As Joe listened to this explana- tion, a limo pulled up, and he rushed out the door, helped the driver with his bags, and they were off to the airport.

William, who was upset that he had arrived late, was detei- mined to make up for lost time. The Belt Parkway had been quite crowded, and William thought he could make better time on a shortcut through some side streets. He was right. Breezing along, Joe finally began to relax, thinking that he might make his plane after all. That's when an oversized yel- low taxi traveling in the opposite direction cut across the yellow line and sideswiped the limo. Had his driver used more caution, Joe said, the limo might have avoided the accident it encountered just five miles from the airport.

Joe was not hurt, but the driver hit his head on the steering wheel and had to be transported to the hospital for observa- tion. Joe, of course, would not leave the scene until the police had completed their report, at which time it was explained that the taxi had swerved over the line to avoid hitting a shop- ping cart that had been pushed into the road by a four-year- old who had been shopping with her mother. Apparently, the child became upset because she had just dropped her ice cream cone, and she had pushed the shopping cart away in frustration as her mother unloaded groceries into their car.

Determined to make *any* flight that night, Joe finally hopped into a cab. He spent the ride mulling over the events he had just been part of, choosing a *what if* approach. *What if William hadn't been listening to the radio station that clued him in to the traffic on the Belt Parkway? What if Paul had been the ninth or the eleventh caller instead of the tenth? What if the limo company had sent a more experienced driver? What if the little girl had not dropped her ice cream cone?* Joe kept

...ing these questions over in his mind as he made his way the airport.

His thoughts quickly faded when he entered the airport terminal. It was evident from the news cameras and overwrought crowd that something had happened. When he saw that most of these people were in tears, Joe realized that whatever had occurred was truly terrible. TWA Flight 800 from New York to Paris had just gone down off the coast of Long Island. At that moment, there was no information about survivors. He overheard some people talking about flight destinations, and he reached for his ticket: *Flight 800*. His knees buckled. Joe was able to make it to a group of chairs and sit down before his legs gave out.

Initially, Joe didn't know what to think, so he watched the scene around him in a daze. He watched the camera people and news reporters. He watched the airline employees, visibly shaken as they tried to perform their jobs. Some were unable to hold back their tears as they tried their best to answer questions and assist the friends and relatives of passengers. "That was the hardest part to watch," Joe said in a still shaky voice, "those poor people and their relatives." Everyone nearby was desperately hoping to hear someone say that everyone on board had been rescued and would be brought back safely.

After the initial shock, Joe's horror transformed into a review of the day's events that had led him to that moment. He went over the mishaps that had prevented him from catching that flight. Obviously no longer angry about missing his plane, he began to feel guilty instead, as if he had somehow cheated death. He then felt amazed and blessed when he reviewed the events that had saved him. He also felt confused and in awe of everything that had happened, which is what had prompted him to call me.

Joe needed to know if he had been "fated" to miss that flight and thus continue to live. He also wanted to know if those two hundred or so strangers on the plane had been

fated to die together in a terrible crash. At two A.M., poor Jo
had come face to face with mankind's most mysterious and
powerful force, *fate.*

After Joe finished spilling forth his terrible story, I attempted
to express my humble understanding of "fate." It just so happened that there was a similar event in my family's history that
helped me understand some of Joe's perplexity. Because the
event did not happen directly to me, it was not as traumatic as
nearly boarding Flight 800 had been for him, but it did prompt
me to give a lot of thought to the meaning of fate as it affects
all of our lives.

In 1912, my grandmother was a young girl in England. Her
family had struggled to obtain tickets to come to America
aboard a large ship. Just like Joe, however, they had the
supreme good fortune to miss the boat, the *Titanic.* Soon after,
they were able to book passage on another ship and eventually
they settled in upstate New York. My grandmother would later
meet my grandfather, they would fall in love, get married, and
have children, one of whom was my father. My father would
grow up and meet and marry my mother . . . and here I am,
writing this sentence today. I have often wondered what would
have happened if my relatives had made it to the boat on time.
Would my grandmother have survived the *Titanic's* sinking?
Would the rest of her family? If she alone had survived, would
she still have made it to upstate New York?

And then, the unthinkable question: What if she hadn't
survived? There would be no son Glenn, no granddaughter
Donna. I have often thanked God for the person who was
unable to get the family to the dock on time in 1912. Was it
a choice he or she made purposefully? Could someone have
known what was to happen? Or did whoever it was simply
spend an extra moment lingering over a cup of tea and lose
track of time?

The fact is, we will never know the answers to these questions. What we can come to know, however, is ourselves. And

s I have attempted to put forth in these pages, if we combine intuition with a deeper understanding of who we are—
made visible to us by the various aspects of personality found
in our own hand—we can change our lives.

Was Joe "fated" to miss his plane and thus continue to live?
As he related his story to me that summer night, I listened to
his struggle to believe that all of the events that had tran-
spired that day were somehow predestined. If I had not lived
a life of "just knowing," or if I had not had the opportunity
to come to comprehend the deeply significant information
that the art of palmistry provides, I might have agreed with
his fatalistic argument.

But fatalism, the belief that events are determined by fate,
is an altogether different idea than the literal meaning of fate.
The Greek word for fate is *moira,* which means "a part of, or
a share of." *Moira* itself derives from *mer,* which means "to
think, ponder, consider, or measure." The Greeks acknowledged, then, that we each have "our lot in life," and rather
than be at the mercy of our circumstances, we can work with
what we have to change those circumstances.

From the Latin, *fatum,* fate has been understood to mean
what has been spoken. I hope that you have come to realize
through these pages that we need only to look at the lines
and markings of our hands for the evidence that the very
course of our lives is written in our flesh. As we strive for a
deeper understanding of who we are, our palms unquestion-
ably reveal that our fate is in our own hands.

Each day of our lives, we begin again. Let us look to our
hands, then, to guide us on life's most precious passage, the
journey to the self. May God bless you and keep you on this
most vital path—the path to intuition.

APPENDIX

Making Your Own Handprint

As mentioned earlier in the book, the *easiest* way to to make a copy of your hand is on a copying machine. The *best* way to view the sometimes slight details of the palm, however, is to make an ink print. Before you begin, you will need to purchase some of the following materials from an art supply store:

a flat pan, cookie sheet, or flat sheet of glass
a tube of black water-soluble ink
a small hand roller, approximately 4½ to 6 inches in size
a small absorbent towel
heavy bond typing paper

To begin, fold the towel into a square that is larger than your hand. Then, center a piece of typing paper over the towel. Squeeze out a thin line of ink onto the pan or dish. Use the roller to work the ink evenly over the pan's surface. Now put your hand gently down onto the inked surface of

241

the pan. When the surface of your palm is completely covered with ink, carefully lift up your hand and gently set it on the paper. Press firmly for a few seconds, then slowly peel the paper from your hand. Allow the page to dry. Wash the ink from your hand with soap and water (that's why it should be water-soluble ink only), then sign and date the print. *Repeat* this procedure every three to six months, or when significant events occur in your life.

BIBLIOGRAPHY

Adler, Mortimer J., and Charles Van Doren. *Great Treasury of Western Thought*. New York: Adler & Van Doren, 1977.

Altman, Nathaniel. *The Palmistry Workbook*. Thorsons Publishing, Aquarian Press, London 1984.

Arcarti, Kristyna. *Spiritual Healing: A Beginner's Guide*. London: Headway-Hodder & Stoughton, 1996.

Aristotle. *Chiromantia*. Ulm, Germany: Johann Reger, 1490.

Aveni, Anthony. *Behind the Crystal Ball: Magic, Science and the Occult from Antiquity through the New Age*. Random House, Times Books, New York 1996.

Aylesworth, Thomas G. *Palmistry*. New York: Franklin Watts, 1976.

Bacher, Elman. *Studies in Astrology, vols. 1 & 2*. Oceanside, CA: Rosicrucian Fellowship, 1962.

Barber, Richard. *A Companion to World Mythology*. New York: Kestrel Books, 1979.

Barry, Theodore J. *The Hand as a Mirror of Systemic Disease*. Philadelphia, PA: F.A. Davis, 1963.

Blake, William. *The Complete Poems of William Blake*. New York: Penguin Books, 1978.

Brau, Jean-Louis; Helen Weaver; and Allan Edmands. *Larousse Encyclopedia of Astrology*. New York: McGraw-Hill, 1977.

Budge, Wallis E.A. *The Egyptian Book of the Dead, The Papyrus of Ani*. New Hyde Park, NY: Citadel Press, 1969.

243

ampbell, Joseph, ed. *The Portable Jung,* trans. by R.F.C. Hall. New York: Viking Press, 1971.

Campbell, Joseph. *The Power of Myth with Bill Moyers,* ed. Betty Sue Flowers. New York: Doubleday, 1988.

Cavendish Jr., Richard, and Yvonne Deutch. *Man, Myth, and Magic, vol. 3.* New York: Marshall, Cavendish, 1983.

Chinmoy, Sri. *Astrology and the Supernatural and the Beyond,* 2nd ed. Hollis, NY: Aum Publications, 1991.

Chopra, Deepak. *The Seven Spiritual Laws of Success.* San Rafael, CA: Amber-Allen Publishing, 1994.

Choquette, Sonia. *The Psychic Pathway.* New York: Crown, 1994.

Combs, Allan, and Mark Holland. *Synchronicity: Science, Myth, and the Trickster,* 2nd ed. New York: Marlowe & Company, 1996.

Constable, George, ed. *Psychic Powers,* Mysteries of the Unknown. New York: Time-Life Books, 1987.

———. *Search for the Soul,* Mysteries of the Unknown. New York: Time-Life Books, 1988.

———. *Spirit Summonings,* Mysteries of the Unknown. New York: Time-Life Books, 1987.

———. *Visions and Prophecies,* Mysteries of the Unknown. New York: Time-Life Books, 1988.

Costavil, Maria. *How to Read Palms.* New York: Crescent Books, 1988.

D'Aulaires, Edgar and Ingrid. *D'Aulaires' Book of Greek Myths.* New York: Doubleday, Delacorte Press, 1965.

Day, Laura. *Practical Intuition.* New York: Random House, Villard Books, 1996.

Edmunds, I.G. *Second Sight: People Who Read the Future.* New York: Thomas Nelson, 1977.

Elahi, Bahram. *The Path of Perfection: The Spiritual Teaching of Nur Ali Elahi,* trans. J.W. Morris. Rockport, ME: Element Books, 1993.

Evans-Wentz, W.Y. *The Tibetan Book of the Dead.* New York: Oxford, 1949.

Flanagan, Beverly. *Forgiving the Unforgivable: Overcoming the Bitter Legacy of Intimate Wounds.* New York: Macmillan, 1992.

Fowler, George. *Learning to Dance Inside: Getting to the Heart of Meditation.* New York: Harcourt Brace, 1996.

Fox, Emmet. *Power Through Constructive Thinking.* New York: HarperCollins, 1989.

Gettings, Fred. *The Book of the Hand.* London: Paul Hamlyn, 1965.

Goldberg, Philip. *The Intuitive Edge: Understanding and Developing Intuition.* Boston: Houghton Mifflin 1983.

Grendahl, Spencer. *Romance on Your Hands.* New York: Simon & Schuster, Fireside, 1990.

Hadingham, Evan. *Early Man and the Cosmos.* New York: Walker & Company, 1984.

Hamilton-Parker, Craig. *Your Psychic Powers: A Beginner's Guide.* London: Headway-Hodder & Stoughton, 1996.

Hand, Robert. *Horoscope Symbols.* Rockport, MA: Para Research, 1981.

Hartleib, Johann. *Die Kunst Chiromantia.* Germany: 1475.

Hipskind, Judith. *Palmistry: The Whole View.* St. Paul, MN: Llewellyn Publications, 1977.

The Holy Bible, King James Version, London: Oxford Univ. Press, 1969.

Hutchinson, Beryl. *Your Life in Your Hands.* London: Sphere Books, 1969.

Journal of the American Medical Association (Dec. 29, 1966.)

Keyes, Ken, Jr. *Handbook to a Higher Consciousness,* 5th ed. Berkeley, CA: Living Love Center, 1976.

Kubler-Ross, Elizabeth. *Death Is of Vital Importance.* Barrytown, NY: Station Hill Press, 1995.

Kushner, Harold S. *How Good Do We Have to Be? A New Understanding of Guilt and Forgiveness.* New York: Little, Brown, 1996.

Levine, Frederick G. *The Psychic Sourcebook.* New York: Warner Books, 1988.

Levine, Stephen. *Meetings at the Edge.* New York: Doubleday, Anchor Press, 1984.

Luxon, Bettina, and Jill Goolden. *Your Hand.* London: Heinemann, 1983.

MacKenzie, Nancy. *Palmistry for Women.* New York: Warner Books, 1973.

Monaghan, Patricia. *The Book of Goddesses and Heroines.* New York: E.P. Dutton, 1981.

Montagu, Ashley. *Touching: The Human Significance of the Skin.* New York: Columbia Univ. Press, 1971.

Morrissey, Mary Manin. *Building Your Field of Dreams.* New York: Bantam Books, 1996.

Moss, Richard. *The Black Butterfly: An Invitation to Radical Aliveness.* Berkeley, CA: Celestial Arts Press, 1986.

Nadall, Florry. *Pen in Hand: A Simplified Guide to "Instant" Handwriting Analysis.* Garden City, NY: Doubleday, 1965.

The New York Public Library. *The Century of American Quotations.* New York: Time Warner, A Stonesong Press Book, 1992.

Pollack, Rachel. *Teach Yourself Fortune Telling.* New York: Henry Holt, 1986.

Scheimann, Eugene, M.D., and Nathaniel Altman. *Medical Palmistry.* London: Thorsons Publishing, Aquarian Press, 1989.

Sheldrake, Rupert. *The Rebirth of Nature: The Greening of Science and God.* New York: Bantam Books, 1991.

Shepard, Leslie, ed. *Encyclopedia of Occultism and Parapsychology.* Secaucus, NJ: Gale Research, 1978.

Signell, Karen A. *Wisdom of the Heart: Working with Women's Dreams.* New York: Bantam Books, 1990.

Sorrell, Walter. *The Study of the Human Hand.* Indianapolis, IN: Bobbs-Merrill, 1967.

Spier, Julius. *The Hands of Children.* London: Routledge & Kegan Paul, 1955.

Steinbach, Martin. *Medical Palmistry: Health and Character in Palmistry.* Secaucus, NJ: University Books, 1975.

Union of International Associations, ed. *Encyclopedia of World Problems and Human Potential,* 3 vols., 4th ed. Belgium: Union of International Associations, 1994–95.

Van de Castle, Robert L. *Our Dreaming Mind.* New York: Ballantine, 1994.

Wilson, Frank. *The Hand.* New York: Random House, 1988.

Wolff, Charlotte. *The Hand in Psychological Diagnosis.* London: Metheun, 1951.

———. *The Human Hand.* New York: Alfred A. Knopf, 1943.

WEB SITES

"Quotes to Inspire You." Online posting. *People's Cyber Nation Page.* 1999. 27 Apr. 1999. <http.//www.cyber-nation/com/victory/ quotations/subjects/quotes>

Read, J.L. "Creative Power of Myth." Online posting. *Enchanted Mind.* 1997. 20 Apr. 1999. <http://enchantedmind.com>

Visit Donna McCue online at http://www.donnamccue.com

ACKNOWLEDGMENTS

From Donna McCue

I want to thank my husband, Larry, for being a true teacher on my path. He has been the light for me, making it possible to see my dreams come true no matter how long it has taken. I also want to thank Linda Chester & Associates for making this book possible and most especially my agent, Joanna Pulcini, who gave me the great gift of her talent and skill from the beginning of this project, her assistant, Peter O'Reilly, who showed kindness and caring during my many phone calls (one day he will be a great author himself), Laurie Fox, and Gary Jaffe, who have all been completely supportive of my book and me.

I am blessed with Emily Heckman, my editor and friend, who has been wonderful during the course of this project. I am in good hands with Emily's wisdom and guidance and am ever grateful for her knowledge and support. Thanks, too, to my publicity team of Pam Duevel, Melinda Mullin, and especially Laura Mullen, for their enthusiasm toward this book and toward me, and to Charlotte Sherwood, for her beautiful illustrations. To Stacey Donovan, my coauthor, I thank you for your talent and writing skill.

To my dear friend Nat Altman, who has always believed in my gift and wanted me to write this book for a long time, I thank you for your support over the past twenty years. Thanks, too, to Patricia Brennan, attorney and friend. To my soul sisters in the creative group, Lainie, Nina, Linda, and Giselle, for all their support, I love you all. And to my real sisters, Debbie and Mary, and my brothers Doug, Dana, Dennis, Darrell, and Danny, for being there. Last and foremost, I want to thank my parents for bringing me into this world.

From Stacey Donovan

Many thanks to everyone at Linda Chester & Associates, especially Joanna Pulcini for her vision of this book, and to Laurie Fox for her expertise. Special thanks to Dennis Dalrymple, for helping this project float when it was otherwise sinking, and to Emily Heckman, whose sharp insight has shaped these pages. Love to the Tuesday girls for lending their ears even when they had heard it all before, and special thanks to Amy Wilkerson for listening when I said, "You won't believe this . . ." I am grateful to Donna Helb and Eleanor Bogart, who provided additional research, and to Charlotte Sherwood, whose illustrations have added an elegance beyond words to this project. Finally, my appreciation for Donna McCue's "just knowing" has only increased while I wrote these pages.

INDEX